D1564776

WHO IS
CHAUNCEY SPENCER?

To Carol Hull
With Warm Regards 'n Best Wishes.

Chauncey E Spencer
14 November 1992
Lynchburg, Virginia

Who Is

Chauncey Spencer?

by

Chauncey E. Spencer

bp

BROADSIDE PRESS
12651 Old Mill Place   Detroit, Michigan 48238

First Edition
First Printing
Copyright © 1975 by Chauncey E. Spencer
All rights reserved

No part of this book can be copied, reproduced or
used in any way without written permission from
Broadside Press, 12651 Old Mill Place
Detroit, Michigan 48238

ISBN: 0-910296-25-1 Cloth $7.95

Manufactured in the U.S.A.

SHERWOOD BRANCH LIBRARY

JUL 1 6 2014

To my two beautiful Anns—
my mother and my wife
and to all my family and friends
who helped to make this book possible.

TABLE OF CONTENTS

INTRODUCTION

WHEN CHAUNCEY E. SPENCER FIRST WALKED into my office and courteously introduced himself, I was rather impressed by this man with spreckled gray hair appearing to be in his early fifties. He informed me that he had been referred to Mr. Randall, owner of Broadside Press, in hopes of publishing his autobiography. Since Mr. Randall was not present, I gave him a receipt for the manuscript and assured him that it would receive careful consideration.

As I glanced at the title of the manuscript, *It Didn't Just Happen Today* . . . I thought: Who is Chauncey Spencer? (This title I would later suggest for the book.)

After reading the autobiography, my question was answered. Chauncey E. Spencer was born and reared in the southern town of Lynchburg, Virginia. He is the son of the famed poet, Anne Spencer; a graduate of Virginia Theological Seminary; a Black pioneer aviator instrumental in the inclusion of Blacks into the Army Air Corps; a member of the Tuskegee Airmen; a civil service official who was awarded the highest civilian service medal only to be branded a Communist during the McCarthy era; the Police Commissioner of San Bernardino, California; and presently the Deputy Administrator for the City of Highland Park, Michigan.

I immediately recognized the value in the historical content of this book, but I also realized that this man's story was representative of additional, more profound values.

9

Chauncey Spencer is a product of those decades of American history which anteceded the Black awareness era of the sixties. He is symbolic of all the Black men who have worked quietly and diligently in the hope of integration, believing and practicing respect, fair play, equal opportunity, equality and justice for all—the American dream.

Many Blacks will be turned off by such lines as: "I'm an American first; a Negro, second." Others will agree with lines such as: "To be called Black might give some so-called Negroes a personal sense of security, but it tags him; it sets him apart. Separate but equal was ruled unconstitutional long ago." However, those who have abandoned the American dream and desire separateness (Blackness), and those who still believe in and desire integration cannot help but reach a consensus on such lines that reveal the true depth of the man: "Let there be no mistake, we need, indeed it is necessary to have, pride in ourselves, our background and our heritage, but not for the sake of blackness itself. Too often, we are mistaking the appearance of pride for the real thing."

Chauncey Spencer is a part of our history, whether one prefers to call it Black or American history. More important, he is that product which portrays the struggle, the suffering, the victories, the progress of all Blacks reared in the ideology of integration in this American society. As his mother, Anne Spencer, wrote about her family in response to a newspaper attack upon her son when he was the Employee Relations Officer at Wright-Patterson Air Force Base: "Yes, we are all average American humans. Folk who work hard; avoid any special limelight when we can do so; respect others as we ourselves demand respect—something to glow about when, save for the Grace of God, we could be putrid."

Chauncey Spencer is a man of principle. Whether his beliefs are right or wrong will only be determined by history. But he has steadfastly practiced and maintained his belief in that one essential element which transcends all societies, races, creeds and colors—human dignity.

—*W. T. Whitsitt*
Broadside Press

CHAPTER ONE

WE LANDED IN A CORN FIELD IN SHERWOOD, Ohio, descending on the land like a giant locust. A farmer, in plaid shirt and overalls, ran across the field towards us. I don't think he'd seen more than one or two Negroes in his entire life. Now here were two in his backyard in an old, two-wing airplane that seemed to be falling apart.

It was May, 1939, a day of high winds and even higher hopes. Convinced we were about to make history, co-pilot Dale White and I had taken off at about six A.M. from Chicago. The plane's top speed was near one hundred ten miles an hour, and whenever we met a heavy wind we'd literally start flying backwards. But that didn't seem important. All that mattered to us was that we were two Negroes flying an airplane in a day and age when many white people believed we couldn't—either because of incompetence, ignorance, or a combination of both. We were bound for Washington, D.C. where we planned to urge Congress to include black pilots in the proposed Civilian Pilot Training program for the Army Air Corps, the predecessor of the Air Force.

But the story of how Dale and I reached the point where we were able to make that flight stretches back in time— maybe back to November 5, 1906—the day I, Chauncey Edward Spencer, was born in the beautiful, rather placid town of Lynchburg, Virginia.

The Lynchburg days I remember were in a South where the peaceful tranquility of sun-lit days was a facade that covered up much hatred and deceit. In this small town of fifty thousand people located in the center of Virginia, a strong undercurrent of racial tensions existed. I eventually became obsessed with the desire just to get away from Lynchburg. It probably started on that clear April day when, at age eleven, I saw my first airplane, one of the first airplanes to ever fly over the city of Lynchburg.

"Woogie, come here," my mother shouted, her firm voice snatching me away from play. "Woogie," my nickname, was given to me shortly after my birth, and it has stuck firmly to this day.

I rushed out to the Virginia hillside on that chill morning in 1917, red clay sticking to my shoes.

"Look up," my mother said, pointing to the steel-blue Virginia sky. An airplane was flying overhead, cutting through the feathery clouds like a knife slicing bread. We could see the news of the event spread from mouth to mouth as neighbors rushed outside for their first glance at an airplane.

I was eleven years old. The very next day I began building my own plane. It was a funny-looking thing. I used a barrel for the fuselage and cockpit, and I covered the wings with old sheets. A wagon was the landing gear carriage for the cockpit and a barrel stave was the propeller. It was odd-looking, but I loved pulling it around the hills. When it built up enough momentum, it would even lift slightly from the ground, making me dream again of my own airplane in the sky. When I was older, my dad helped me build an airplane with a gasoline motor. Flying was a dream every man and boy could engage in at the time. With me, though, this dream stayed even into adulthood, despite my mother's wish for me to be a "gentleman farmer."

Although as a child I had no knowledge of the heavy odds against any Negro aspiring to become a pilot, I sensed that my dreams were spun of fragile hopes. My boyhood life in Lynchburg, for the most part, was pleasant at this time. Sometimes it was even exciting for me, my parents "Mr. Ed" and "Miss Anne," and my two sisters: Bethel, five years older than myself and Alroy, three years older. My father was prominent in town as his father was before him. Grandad, "Pappy," owned the first Maxwell automobile in Lynchburg. Dad first owned a grocery store with his brother; then he had a Post Office job, making a lucrative $1,000-$1,200 in 1910. They also made numerous investments in real estate, buying lots, 100 x 180, "two for a quarter," meaning two lots for twenty-five dollars.

My father was also responsible for the city's first private housing development, which became known as Spencer Place. Here, in as many as fourteen houses at one time lived most of my relatives. We were surrounded by them. In my boyhood, at least, I led the life of a typical Negro child. However, our better financial situation and our culture-pervaded home was not that of many of the Negro families. Our family was not poor, but not rich—working people.

My mother, Anne Spencer, was and still is, though into her nineties, a very cultured woman. Librarian, teacher, and noted poet, she was closely associated with some of the leading Negroes in the country. She is a racial mixture of Irish, Negro and Seminole Indian. For many years, my mother was the librarian at our local high school. She is also a published poet, her works appearing in various anthologies. Many well-known Negroes made frequent trips to Lynchburg to discuss the important issues of the day with my parents.

Among her other qualities, my mother was a woman of high integrity and principle. She was born in Henry County near Danville, Virginia. Even though she was aware of the fact she was born in Virginia, Mother later listed her birthplace as Bramwell, West Virginia, 1882. Her reason for this was one of principle, Virginia had once been a slave state and West Virginia was not. My mother received most of her education in West Virginia. She went to college at Virginia Seminary and College in Lynchburg where she met my father. She always said about the matter of Virginia, "Virginia is a great state. This is where democracy was born. It died here, too!"

Mother has allowed me to use the following poem:

13

AT THE CARNIVAL
by Anne Spencer

Gay little Girl-of-the-Diving-Tank,
I desire a name for you,
Nice, as a right glove fits:
For you—who amid the malodorous
Mechanics of this unlovely thing,
Are darling of spirit and form.
I know you—a glance, and what you are
Sits-by-the-fire in my heart.
My Limousine-Lady knows you, or
Why does the slant-envy of her eye mark
Your straight air and radiant inclusive smile?
Guilt pins a fig-leaf; Innocence is its own adorning.
The bull-necked man knows you—this first time
His itching flesh sees form divine and vibrant health
And thinks not of his avocation.
I came incuriously—
Set on no diversion save that my mind
Might safely nurse its brook of misdeeds
In the presence of a blind crowd.

The color of life was gray.
Everywhere the setting seemed right
For my mood.
Here the sausage and garlic booth
Sent unholy incense skyward;
There a quivering female-thing
Gestured assignations, and lied
To call it dancing;
There, too, were games of chance
With chances for none;
But oh! Girl-of-the-Tank, at last!
Gleaming Girl, how intimately pure and free
The gaze you send the crowd,
As though you know the dearth of beauty
In its sordid life.
We need you—my Limousine-Lady,
The bull-necked man and I.

14

Seeing you here brave and water-clean,
Leaven for the heavy ones of earth,
I am swift to feel that what makes
The plodder glad is good; and
Whatever is good is God.
The wonder is that you are here;
I have seen the queer places,
But never before a heaven-fed
Naiad of the Carnival-Tank!
Little Diver, Destiny for you,
Like as for me, is shod in silence;
Years may seep into your soul
The bacilli of the usual and the expedient;
I implore Neptune to claim his child to-day!

There were visitors to our home like George Washington
Carver, Paul Robeson, James Weldon Johnson, Walter
White, Clarence Muse, Dean Pickens, and W. E. B. DuBois.
They talked about the theater, literature, the NAACP.
Adam Clayton Powell talked mostly about himself when he
came to visit just after he married Isabelle. He had wanted
a hideaway for his honeymoon and had made arrangements,
through Reverend Vernon Johns, with my uncle who lived
next door to us to use his house. I can recall him joking
about how the Abyssinian Baptist Church had given his new
wife a seven thousand dollar mink coat and a five thousand
dollar cash gift to honeymoon in Trinidad in Jamaica. And
here he was in Lynchburg, Virginia.

Langston Hughes visited our home in 1927. He enjoyed
discussing poetry with my mother, but he also talked about
civil rights efforts he was involved in back in Harlem. During the 1920's he and others fought for Negro employment
by white store owners around 125th Street. This fight extended on into the 1930's. At long last their fight was successful, and stores took on Negro workers.

With great disappointment Hughes told of an experience
he had shortly after the first barrier was broken. One day
he went to a 5 & 10 store in the neighborhood to buy a ball

15

of twine. Two Negro girls were working there as sales clerks. When he came to the counter, they continued their lively conversation ignoring him as he stood waiting.

Hughes finally said, "I'd like to buy this; would you please wait on me?"

One of the girls turned around and rudely said, "Just wait a minute; I'll be there in awhile."

With that remark, Hughes became angry. He threw the ball of twine down and said, "Goddamn it; this is what I worked for!" At that he walked out in disgust.

Writing to my mother after this visit, Hughes said, "I was sorry to go away and leave my primroses, but maybe they will grow and be there the next time I come down. Lynchburg was very good to me I thought. I had a great time. . . . I sent you my sonnets this afternoon. Please think about them as poems not as sonnets, because maybe they aren't the last."

Another influential who stayed at the Spencer home was Thurgood Marshall. In 1925 and 26, Thurgood was chief attorney for the NAACP. The work of the NAACP was so great that he was particularly upset when people came to him with trivial issues and charges. One time he told us about a small town in Mississippi. The Negro citizens sent a complaint to the NAACP to bring suit against the local government for not allowing them to enter the city park or the city zoo. Marshall decided to go to Mississippi to investigate. What he found there amazed him. The general condition of the white section of town was poor, with run-down houses and without sidewalks. However, on the other side of the tracks there were not even sewage systems or running water. Most of the people were living in shacks and leantos.

Thurgood asked us, "How can these people be so concerned about the city park and zoo when they don't even have decent homes to live in or sanitary systems to prevent disease?"

Of all of them, I think I was most impressed by Paul Robeson. I remember thinking that Robeson was a man who didn't need a door, who could walk through a wall. He

16

was a broad-shouldered, dignified man who looked like a giant—at least to a child. Little did I know at the time that it would be my presence at a rally featuring Paul Robeson that would later be the cause for my being regarded as a "security risk" by the government.

Mother never hero-worshipped any of the visitors, however. She was too down-to-earth and practical for that. She wouldn't mince words about anyone, no matter who they were. Sometimes, to my chagrin, I inherited this trait from her. I remember once asking her what she thought of W. E. B. DuBois. "He simply set the words down," she said. "He really made less sacrifices than others because of his superior intelligence. He's too intolerant of anyone who isn't just like himself."

Anne Spencer had a caustic tongue. I recall once visiting a monument that read "George Washington slept here." My mother replied: "He slept with a lot of Black women, too!" When she felt wronged, there were no sacred cows. My mother was full of fire, particularly on racial issues. She was always writing letters to the editor pointing to improvements needed in Lynchburg. Sometimes she went a step further than writing.

Once at a meeting in Merchant's Hall where a political candidate was attempting to brainwash an all Negro audience, mother sat there patiently. During the question and answer period, mother asked, "Just why should we really give you our vote? I really see no difference between you and the other candidate." His reply was, "Because I'm telling you all I'm better!" Mother said but one word, "Shit," an outspoken pronouncement for any woman of the 1920's. The meeting ended abruptly on that note.

Most of it had very little meaning to me as a boy, although mother's dogged determination was an example to me when I later needed that same kind of persistence or be swallowed in racial injustice. It was not long before I had my first brush with the fires that had scorched my mother.

Lynchburg, like many aristocratic Southern towns, had no residential segregation. Negroes and whites lived side by side, played together, laughed and chatted on still, hot nights

17

when the air seemed heavy with mutual memories. There was none of the open antagonism of the rural "red neck" areas of the South. On Sundays, we went to different churches and during the week to different schools, but that, somehow, seemed natural and fitting. It was the way things were and had always been.

Then things began to happen in Lynchburg. Small, troubling things. A new teacher, Miss Ora, came to our school. She was one of our first Negro high school teachers. Until this time, we had had all white teachers at our all-Negro high school. Miss Ora couldn't have been more than four feet ten inches tall. Perhaps she tried to compensate in impact what she lacked in size. I think it was she who stimulated the first feelings of racism among the student body. She would strut, Napoleonesque in stance, into the classroom and call out: "Who's that talkin' over there? When I find out who's talkin', I'm going to take 'em downtown to the white folks and they'll take care of him."

Or, she would say, "If I ever see you doing that again, I'm goin' to call the white folks. They'll put you in your place."

Her persistent references to white folks and what they would do to us began to have an effect. Inevitably, we became more conscious of racial feelings and the separation between us and our lighter-skinned peers. Fights between Negro and white school children began to break out. The authorities at the white school finally had to arrange it so that the white children were sent home fifteen minutes earlier than the Negro children. Parents warned their children to, "Leave those other kids alone. Don't bother with them. Everybody's looking for trouble."

In all justice to Miss Ora, I would have to give her credit, too. She was an innovative teacher who brought ballet classes and a credit system for lunches to our school. If a child couldn't afford to pay for his salmon sandwiches and johnny cakes that the older students made, she could credit it to a charge account to be paid at the end of the week. Miss Ora's references to the white folks were simply her way of maintaining control of the class and, after all, this is what she had been taught, too.

My real run-in with Miss Ora came when I was twelve years old and in the seventh grade. A typical school boy prank of the day was to stick a pin in your shoe so that it protruded out the front. I had stuck the pin in my shoe and was threatening to stick the girl next to me.

"Miss Ora, Chauncey stuck me with a pin," lamented the girl.

"I did not. I was only pretendin' to."

It was too late, though. Miss Ora's fury took its toll in blows rather than words. The small teacher struck at me with a yardstick but, this time, I caught hold of it and hit her back, once, across the arm. She was too shocked to say or do anything more. She recoiled, left the room and wasn't seen the remainder of the day. I, too, was equally perplexed. I certainly hadn't anticipated hitting her but I had a temper, then, as I do now, and I wasn't going to let her get away with beating me for something I didn't even do. I was sent home from school by Miss LeGrand, the white principal, to my mother's verbal whiplash, a fate worse than the yardstick. My parents were genuinely concerned about my behavior and where it would lead me. They even had Reverend Lord O. Lewis, our minister and longtime friend, talk to me at length about self-discipline and the need to control my emotions.

All of these things were small, dark clouds that had a cumulative effect by the time I was nearing thirteen years of age. One day, I packed my bags and went down to the railroad station, determined to run away to Washington. I left a note saying, "I don't want to live in a city with this hatred." I was apprehended before the train arrived—the ticket agent knew me and called my father. I was easily persuaded to return home.

Not that I gave up my pranks, however! I was a daring kid who'd climb tall ladders and walk around the narrow edge of construction sites, perhaps three hundred feet from the ground. No amount of telling me to be careful could deter my restlessness.

19

I was enterprising, too. One day while visiting my aunt Marietta at nearby Randolph Macon women's college, I noticed that Miss Ida, head of the kitchen, was throwing away all the chicken giblets.

"Don't you use those? Can I have 'em?"

"Well, sure, Woogie, but what are you going to do with them?"

"I'll sell them." And sell them I did. Twice a week I'd go to the college and get my forty to fifty pounds of gizzards, load them in my wagon and sell them house to house. Ten cents a pound for chicken feet. Twenty cents a pound for the heart, liver and gizzards. That kept me in pocket money until I was fourteen years old.

When I was fourteen, I got a delivery and clerking job in Reid's pharmacy located on Fifth Street, about eight blocks from my home. The area behind Reid's pharmacy was referred to as the "Black Bottom" because of its heavy Negro population. It also surrounded a "red light district" laden with white prostitution. Because of my frequent drugstore deliveries there, I had direct contact with the houses and became well-acquainted with the occupants. Sodas, medicine, liquor—whatever Doc Reid sent— I delivered. I got to know the madams and their call girls very well. They'd invite me in to talk and I, a fourteen-year-old, was entranced. The heavy make-up, the suggestive, gaudy dress— it didn't matter to me that many of them were really not very good looking. To me, they were beautiful. My parents never suspected that the druggist, a community stalwart, would expose me to this kind of situation. And I, sure as hell, wasn't going to tell them.

It was the time of prohibition and liquor could only be obtained with a physician's prescription. Our drugstore's pharmacist had a working relationship with the Negro physicians in town and began an exchange of favors. He would give the physicians wholesale prices on supplies and other "special" favors in exchange for liquor prescriptions. He saved them by the stacks so he could supply his customers at the houses of prostitution. It wasn't long before an associate of his began calling him the nickname that stuck, "Dr.

Swipe." His operation was an early lesson for me in how to get an easy dollar.

There was another lesson I was learning at that time. The white prostitutes catered only to a white clientele from Monday through Friday. On weekends, when the white men were spending time with their families, the Negro "big shots" and professional men began frequenting the houses for their own pleasures. By the time I was sixteen years old and the initial attraction was beginning to wear, I resented the fact that the whites had set up their business in a predominantly Negro area, the only overwhelmingly Negro area in Lynchburg.

Many years later, I talked to an old gilrfriend from Lynchburg who said that as a kid she'd look at the painted ladies as she went to school and think, "That's exactly what I want to be when I grow up." Happenings in the "Fourth Street District" were the subjects of much discussion and laughter among the neigborhood children. Perhaps it was the children's curiosity that began to concern my parents.

There was a growing community awareness of the problem, and I, personally, grew to resent those upstanding community leaders who were guests in our home, and who then went through the back door to the prostitutes.

My own resentment was further heightened by occurences like the one I experienced when on a delivery to Miss Loretta, a prostitute. I walked up to the door, passed the porch's grill-lattice work, the overt sign of prostitution, rather than any actual red light. The lattice work on either side of the porch prevented passers-by from getting a good view of the clientele who might be on the porch. Medicine in hand, I rang the bell. A burly white man, tucking in his shirt, strode down the stairs. Angered by my interruption, he called out, "What the hell's this nigger doin' here?" Young as I was, I was wise enough to choke back the heated words that rose to my lips—knowing that if any trouble with the white man should occur, the guilt would automatically be mine. I wished desperately to learn how to respond, sensing, even then, that there would be many times in the future when my race would be hurled as an epithet against me.

Not long after that I had two experiences that affected me deeply. Both of them occurred in New York. When I was fourteen years old, my parents sent me by train to visit my sisters who were attending Hunter College. They were not there to meet me at the train station, so I asked someone at the information desk where I could get a sandwich. I was directed across the street from Pennsylvania Station. "Child's Restaurant" the big white porcelain letters read. I walked in and sat down at the counter. Fifteen minutes passed and still no waitress had taken my order. Customers who had come in after me were already finished with their sandwiches. Oblivious to the real cause of my failure to be waited on, I walked up to the cashier. "When's a waitress going to take my order?" I innocently asked, thinking they must be either terribly slow or unusually busy.

"We don't serve your people in here."

Suddenly sensitive to the darkness of my skin, I quickly looked around the room to see who had heard her statement. Apparently, no one had, as they continued eating their meals. My voice took on a guarded tone as I noticed the twenty or so white patrons. "Why don't you? I just want a sandwich."

"We don't serve colored people." No answer. Just a re-iteration.

And now the manager was at her side. "If you don't get out of here, I'll have you arrested." Loud and clear. There was no saving myself from the eyes of the other customers now. They were all watching.

"What the hell is this? All's I want is a sandwich. Who the hell do you think you are? You goddamn sonofabitch."

"You're not getting anything here. Now, get out. Out, I said."

"Listen, mister, if I don't get waited on, I'll . . ." but my voice trailed off. Another man was striding from the kitchen to the cashier.

"Need some help with this boy here? I'll give you exactly five seconds to get out through that door." His lumbering frame heaved a step forward as he uttered the final words.

22

Flanked, out-manuevered, I retreated towards the door. As I was going out through the door, the manager had the last say—he shoved me through the door knocking my suitcase out into the street. I picked it up but I didn't dare turn around. I could feel the stares of the customers in the restaurant's large front window.

Angry, ashamed, but not beaten yet, I walked down the block to a second restaurant, but before I was even able to reach a table I was quickly told, "No coloreds, here." I turned and left as if I hadn't heard a thing—before an argument could arise.

In Lynchburg, I couldn't be served at all the restaurants either. But there I knew which ones would only serve Negroes in their special place in the back of the kitchen. I wouldn't think of going to Lynchburg's Piedmont Restaurant or White House unless I went through the back door the kitchen help used. But here in New York I had thought things were different. The North wasn't supposed to have that kind of discrimination. After all, didn't my sisters come home from New York with glowing tales of life there? "New York is worse than Lynchburg. Nobody talks to me like that in Lynchburg," I later told my sisters. The myth of the North's liberalism exploded in my mind with the force of a bursting balloon.

But on the positive side, something happened in New York which lifted my sights and strengthened my hopes. I saw Marcus Garvey. Garvey was the first nationalist and was saying in the 1920's all the things which again became popular with disillusioned Negroes in the 1960's. As the founder of the Universal Negro Improvement Association, Garvey was talking in the 1920's about black pride, black heroes and the need for Negroes to become economically strong. In the early 1920's the UNIA reached its zenith of popularity. Even at my young age I recognized the truth in what Garvey was saying.

"Up, you mighty race, you can accomplish what you will. . . . The Negro of yesterday has disappeared from the scene of human activities and his place is taken by a new Negro who stands erect, conscious of his manhood rights and fully determined to preserve them at all costs." Garvey thundered when he spoke, letting his flowing robes sway. I shall never forget the plumed hat he wore or the supreme confidence he displayed. To some, he was flamboyant and exploitive but he was strong among the people—they showed their support in hard-earned pennies, nickels and dimes. Millions of Negroes, particularly the impoverished in the large cities, rallied to his call for unity and pride. He led the most successful, massbased Negro movement.

I was excited and inspired by Marcus Garvey and I think it is indicative of this country that he, like Paul Robeson, was beaten down to his knees—in Garvey's case by a charge of mail fraud. Thousands of Negroes had bought shares in his Black Star Line, a company designed to show the worth of self improvement, particularly in Negro business activities. The company went bankrupt and Garvey was sent to the federal penitentiary in Atlanta.

At the time, his speech plus the restaurants' refusal of service had a great impact on me. I returned to Lynchburg wiser in the ways of the world and more determined than ever to fulfill my childhood desire to fly. Negroes, if they were ever going to get anywhere, could not accept the status quo.

CHAPTER TWO

IN PRACTICAL TERMS NO FLYING CAREER SEEM-
ed possible. Lynchburg had textile mills, print shops, florists,
bakeries, and other small industries, but that was all. So,
temporarily putting off my more ambitious plans, I got
another local job lasting through my junior and senior years
of high school. This time I was a bell hop at the Hotel Carrol.

It was still during the time of prohibition, and though I
was only a little older than when I worked for Doctor Swipe,
I felt well-schooled in the bootlegging and prostitution busi-
sess, knowledge of which was necessary to a bell hop.

During my first week of work at the hotel, I received a
call to deliver ice water to one of the rooms. The man in the
room asked me, confidentially, to get him some liquor. I
feigned ignorance; we were trained to act naive. He persuaded me to try to find someone who could. I left the
room and discussed the prospect with my contact, the chief
of bell hops, and he agreed we could take a chance. After I
delivered the liquor, the man flashed his badge; he was a
federal agent. He made me identify myself by name and
number and then he called downstairs to verify my employment. He said he would be willing to forget the incident if
I would do him another favor—get him a girl. "I don't care
if she's a nigger gal," he added. I hesitated, this time wonder-

25

ing if I should get out now or get in deeper. I checked again with the Chief and again we decided to take a chance.

I called to the Fourth Street District, on my old drugstore delivery route, and made arrangements for Big Mammie to make the call. About half an hour after Big Mammie's girl, Georgia, arrived, I was summoned to the room. Blanket pulled up to her neck, Georgia was in bed, and the agent was, unashamedly, walking around in his opened bathrobe. He called me by number, "Hey, number four," he said, "you did a good job. You know, every now and then I have to pitch one, and whenever I come here I want you to get my liquor for me—and when I need a girl like Georgia over here, I want you to get her, too." He handed me fifteen dollars which I stuffed into my pocket.

He came once every two or three weeks for several months. If he arrived on Wednesday or Thursday, he'd get so drunk he would be literally on his hands and knees. He never wanted a girl when he reached this stage. But by Monday morning he was as straight and sober as any executive should be.

This was an early lesson for me in the duplicity of some well-established people. But in some ways I, too, was forced to lead a dual life. Although I knew it was wrong, I couldn't resist the money involved in procuring girls for the hotel customers. And, after all, my job depended on it. I could always count on getting ten dollars for my services or sometimes a generous twenty-five, and when a girl was involved for a weekend, she always tipped ten or twelve dollars, a healthy sum of money in the 1920's. I didn't have to sell myself cheaply in this business. Quickly learning to stall the men, to say that all the girls were busy, I knew my fee would increase as the men realized that either they would pay a high price for my services or their one night's fling would be forever lost. "I just can't get anybody tonight. They're all booked up. Sorry, there's no chance," I would say. The distress in the man's face would be obvious. His long-awaited opportunity might be lost. And soon my fee would skyrocket, once as high as one hundred dollars.

This is how many Negroes began careers as pimps—by

26

realizing how lucrative it could be to have ten or twelve men regularly depending on them for their girls. My association with this procurement was limited to the time I worked at the hotel, but it was far more lucrative than the fifteen dollars I earned every two weeks as a bell hop.

The hotel also had a working relationship with the police department selling them bootlegged whiskey. We were often asked to send eight or ten pints of liquor to the officers. One of the chief vice-officers of the police department was closely tied in with bootlegging and prostitution in Lynchburg. The hotel management not only knew of the bootlegging business but actively participated in it. As bell hops, we were allowed one dollar and fifty cents for every bottle of whiskey sold; the rest of the money was turned over to the chief bell hop who, in turn, turned it over to the manager.

During this time of my life, when I was seventeen and eighteen years old, I myself participated in many excursions across the color line. I spent several weekends with white college girls from nearby women's colleges. It started when a friend, an elevator operator in a large department store, met a couple of the girls who wanted "to meet a couple of fellows." He told me they wanted to get together with us. Soon, we'd be picking the girls up in cars and going out to The Lake, a Negro-operated dance hall with a lake and cabins in the woods. As many as fifteen to twenty girls were involved at one time.

When I finished at the all-Negro Dunbar High School, I went to Virginia Theological Seminary, an all-Negro Baptist College where I attended for four years and received a sociology degree. In June of 1927, at age twenty-one, I impulsively married Elvira Jackson, my high school sweetheart. We were both immature, and the marriage lasted only a few years.

Pressed by the need to support a wife, I looked for work but could find only sporadic, odd jobs. The Great Depression was just beginning and jobs were scarce. For every job vacancy, dozens of men lined up to be interviewed. The depression was a great leveler, reducing men and women from all walks of life to wary competitors, each hoping to beat the others out in the contest for employment of any kind. No job was too menial for a man or woman to guard a precious place near the front of the ever-present line of job seekers. I looked everywhere for employment. Finally I found it— the hard way.

Riding up to an intersection at Fifth and Pierce Streets one day, I saw a friend of mine, Eugene Anderson, a truck driver for a wholesale grocery company, collide with a car and kill a child with the company truck. I dashed down to the A. S. White and Company, told them about the accident, told them their driver was being held by the police, and got his job. Salary: $12.50 per week.

After that job, I worked for nine months assisting in social work with the Federal Emergency Relief Administration in Lynchburg, quitting in 1932 to manage a Negro theater, the first non-segregated theater in Lynchburg. Prior to the opening of the Harrison Theater, all other theaters were Jim Crow. Since many Negroes did not want to sit in the galleries while whites enjoyed ground-floor seats, many Negroes had never been to the theater.

Management of the Harrison was a good opportunity for me, but it didn't fulfill the need I had for a more challenging job. That dream of becoming a pilot was still ever-present. It festered in the back of my mind like a sore waiting to be treated. I was beginning to feel that time had perhaps passed me by. I was twenty-seven years old and hadn't even begun my chosen career.

Finally, a door opened. Oscar De Priest, the Chicago Congressional Representative, visited my family and suggested I come to Chicago to study flying, but I wasn't able to take him up on his offer just then. Marital problems kept me rooted to Lynchburg. A year or two later, I accepted his offer. Prompted by a separation from my wife and a pending divorce, I wanted to get away from Lynchburg. Now was my long-awaited opportunity.

By the time I got to Chicago, the opportunity had somewhat diminished. I looked up Oscar De Priest who said, "Oh, you came at the wrong time. Things are bad now. Depression, you know." Receiving little support there, I went to visit the John Robinson School of Aviation. I sensed something was wrong when I walked into the garage. There were two car engines, an aircraft propellor, but nothing that resembled an aircraft school. Colonel Robinson seemed eager for my nine hundred dollars that my father had given me to study but, leary of the school, I left.

I persevered, though, and in 1934 I met Dr. Earl Renfroe, a Negro dentist and flyer. He told me about Chicago's Aeronautical University, which I eagerly sought out. I talked to one of the administrators there who tried to discourage me from attending their classes. The classes were made up of all white students and, "It just wouldn't work out for you to attend." Having come this close to my dream, I wasn't to be turned away that easily, and I finally persuaded the administrator to accept my one hundred dollars in exchange for permission to begin the classes.

The next day, I had attended classes for only two hours when I was called to the office and was told that it wasn't working out, that the white students in school had objected, and that they threatened to leave school if I returned to any more classes. The administrator was still willing to help me and urged me to seek out some Negro instructors at the Coffey School of Aviation who were giving flight training lessons on the South side of Chicago. If they would give me instructions, Aeronautical University would give me their seal of approval upon completion of satisfactory work, he said. So that is what I did and received Aeronautical University's letter of endorsement upon the completion of my work with the Negroes.

The man who introduced me to Aeronautical University, Dr. Earl Renfroe, also introduced me to Dale White, a pioneer Negro flyer. The two of us began rebuilding a plane for the doctor. Years earlier, Dale had gone to all-Negro night classes at Aeronautical University and had then gotten his aircraft engine mechanic's certificate, and later his private pilot's license. He had been flying for four years when I met him.

While taking classes at the Coffey School, I had found a job in the Chicago Loop washing dishes and was flying at

Chicago's Harlem Airport. Over a period of three or four weeks, I would scrape together the twenty-five dollars an hour it cost to fly. The expense was exorbitant, especially considering that because of either engine trouble, sputtering, or weather conditions, it sometimes took the airplane half an hour to get off the ground. None of that mattered, though. I was willing to eat the cheap meals at North Shoreline Restaurant and skimp on the money my father sent to me. The important thing was that I was beginning—in more ways than one—to get off the ground.

I received my student's pilot's license, which did permit me to fly solo but not carry passengers, which I did anyway. No one paid any attention to the "colored boys" at the airport as long as we kept our place and were not too conspicuous.

I couldn't be entirely optimistic, though; past experience with racial discrimination wouldn't allow too much hope. I knew that the public's attitude was extremely hostile to Negro flyers. Repeatedly, I heard, "You'll never get a job flying," and this was said with good reason. The Negro flyers I knew were all supporting themselves with other kinds of jobs. Nobody wanted a Negro pilot, including the armed services. Negroes were not allowed into the training program for the Army Air Corps. It was 1939, the year the famous Charles Lindbergh published an article in *Reader's Digest* in which he called flying ". . . a tool specially shaped for Western hands . . ." But there was hope in the wind. It was also the year in which a group of determined Negro pilots formed the National Airmen's Association. Together, perhaps, we could effect a change.

The National Airmen's Association's main problem was attracting attention. If we were to be more than a mere club of some twenty-or-so Negro flyers, we'd have to gain some public attention for our cause. We finally decided to put on airshows, which proved to be a wise choice. In October, 1938, more than twenty-five thousand spectators crowded into Chicago's Harlem Airport at 187th Street and Harlem Avenue to watch our pilots do their loops, wing-overs, barrel rolls, power dives and spirals.

One of the feature attractions was a parachute race between a white student pilot, Sid Rubin, and myself. Both of us were to bail out of our airplanes; the winner being the one to first reach the ground. It was a bit of a daredevil adventure; jumpers were often hurt as their parachutes failed to open or as they waited too long to pull their rip cord or as their shroud cords fouled. I was enthusiastic. It was thrilling to hurl down from the plane at a rate of one hundred fifty feet per second. The pilot took us up ten thousand feet and we bailed out. The *Chicago Defender*, a Negro newspaper, read: "It was Spencer's fourth leap and in beating Rubin back to earth by fully five minutes from an elevation of over two and a half miles, the Lynchburg youth bailed out and plummeted nearly two miles of the distance without pulling his rip cord. Spectators held their breaths as Spencer hurtled downward, his body describing thin tiny arcs in the course of the fall. It was not until the chute blossomed out above Spencer barely 1,200 feet from the ground that watchers found their voices and let go with lusty cheers." Both of us landed, though, so far from the airstrip that no winner could be declared. The crowd loved us all the same. Their anticipation of adventure was fulfilled as they watched, vicariously experiencing the thrill of the descension.

Buoyed by our first success, we couldn't be stopped now. Dale White and I, sponsored by the NAA and the *Chicago Defender*, rented an airplane and set out on a goodwill tour of ten cities. We put on an airshow wherever we stopped, making an impressive scene as we two, young, handsome, athletic-looking pilots stepped from our plane. The tour was designed to stimulate interest in the first national Negro airshow to be held in Chicago. Enoch P. Waters, Jr., city editor of the *Chicago Defender*, suggested we climax our tour by going to Washington, D.C. to urge our Congressional representatives to push for the inclusion of the Negro in the Army Air Corps.

The idea took hold and we decided to carry it out. That was the birth of what surely must have been one of the most unusual flights ever made by pilots anywhere.

One thousand dollars for the flight was put up by the

celebrated Jones brothers of Chicago who had made much of their money from "policy," a form of the numbers game. Two months after our flight, we showed our appreciation for their donation by flying low over the Jones' estate in the Southern part of Illinois and dropping a bouquet of white flowers and a note of thanks right at their front porch.

We'd been refused any financial help by local organizations. But with the money the Jones brothers donated, plus the five hundred dollars I had saved, we were able to rent an airplane. It was a Lincoln-Paige bi-plane with dual cockpits, one behind the other, and no instruments other than oil pressure and air speed. At this time there were few regulations regarding air safety. Any landing that permitted the flyers to walk away from the plane was considered a good landing.

We took off from Chicago, but after only four hours of flight, we threw a crankshaft. The plane started bucking and we were forced to land in Sherwood, Ohio, in a farmer's backyard. Without any brakes on the plane, we swerved and slid and finally rested within a hundred yards of the farmer's barn. The farmer stared in disbelief at the cream and red plane sitting in his field.

Overcoming his initial shock, he couldn't do enough for us. I think we were probably the most exciting thing that had ever happened to him and Sherwood, Ohio. He took us into town and got us a room in a hotel above a restaurant. Lacking the proper equipment, we'd have to wait until the next day to try to repair the plane. But the next morning the news of our impromptu arrival had spread throughout the small community as well as the nation's wire service and radio. Most of the townspeople came to the corn field to see us and our plane. They crowded around us asking question after question. "Where were you going?" "How did you become a pilot?" "Can only two people fit in there?" And, of course, the inevitable, "Can I have a ride?" A novelty like this sparked everyone's interest. Children, men and women alike were all equally enthused. They were a gracious group of people who paid all our expenses while we were there. To show our appreciation, Dale White and I returned a few months later to spend the day giving the townspeople plane rides and taking their picture in the plane.

But we still had the problem of getting to Washington. We wired the NAA for money. It took them two days to raise fifty-four dollars for a new crankshaft. We worked to repair the airplane in the barn the farmer lent us. After two days, we were anxious to get "Old Faithful," a misnomer for sure, up into the air again.

We resumed our flight, but continued to have a few other minor mishaps. As one of the local newspapers reported: "They continued to Pittsburgh via Morgantown, West Virginia. At Morgantown, dusk was descending. They endeavored to remain there overnight. Air field attendants, after refusing to rent them hangar space, finally sold them some gas with the admonition—'Pittsburg is only fifty-five miles away.' No lights on their ship . . . miles to go . . . and suddenly the curtain of darkness is completely down. The beacon of the Allegheny County Airport guided them on their way. Arriving at the field, they were just about to glide in for a landing, when they spotted a Pennsylvania-Central Airlines transport going in ahead of them. And here it was that they used a bit of headwork. Landing on a strange (and busy) airport in the dark is a ticklish job. So they followed the floating, white tail of the airliner right onto the ground . . . at a safe distance, of course."

The Civil Aeronautics Inspectors had other ideas about a "safe distance." We were temporarily grounded by the inspector for flying too close and endangering the lives of passengers on a commercial airline; however, luck stayed close to us. Robert L. Vann, publisher of the *Pittsburgh Courier* appeared with us and we were cleared the next morning to fly on to Washington.

In Washington, we were met by National Airmen's Association lobbyist, Edgar Brown, also head of the Negro Federal Workers Employees Union. He was called The Goat because he was willing to take on anything or anyone. He took us on the underground train connecting the Capitol and Congressional offices. As we were getting off the electric car, Harry S. Truman, then a Senator from Missouri, came

33

walking down the corridor. Brown intercepted him to introduce us and explain our mission to Washington. Truman was interested and in his customarily direct, blunt way asked many questions.

"What do you do?" he questioned. We explained that we were both working for the WPA.

"So what are you doing here? Why aren't you working today?" We told him we had taken time off because we felt we had to dramatize the need for the inclusion of the Negro in the Army Air Corps.

"Why aren't you in the Air Corps? Can't you get in?" He seemed genuinely surprised. Edgar Brown explained to him that Negroes were not accepted.

"Have you tried?"

"No, sir, but others have tried and have just been embarrassed. They've been turned away without regard for their training or ability. Only the color of their skin mattered."

"Well, I think *you* should try."

"We'd like to try but we'd also like for you to help us open the door. We haven't been able to break down the barriers ourselves. Mr. Truman, you don't know what it means to be embarrassed. I've tried these things before. There's just no use," Dale replied.

"I've been embarrassed before."

"Not like this, Mr. Truman. Not like we are."

Truman had spunk; he wanted to see our plane and arranged to come to the airport that afternoon. He was full of questions as he climbed up on the wing and looked into the cockpit. "How much gas can this carry? How much did it cost to rent? Do you have insurance?" He was enthusiastic, though he didn't want a plane ride. We had our flight suits on, ready to take him up if he wanted a ride. They were khaki jumpsuits of our own design. He said that if we had guts enough to fly this thing to Washington, he'd have enough guts to back us. And he did just that, helping put through legislation insuring that Negroes would be trained along with whites under the Civilian Pilot Training Program.

Along with other officials, we also met Congressman

Everett Dirksen who later introduced the amendment to the Civil Aeronautics bill in the House of Representatives prohibiting discrimination in administration of the benefits of the act. It wasn't until three years later that a bill was passed including Negroes in the Army Air Corps.

Even Eleanor Roosevelt was enthusiastic about this particular cause. One of the newspapers shows a picture of Mrs. Roosevelt getting into a plane with a Negro flyer. Smiling, holding her ubiquitous, flowered hat in hand, she climbed aboard. The newspaper reads: "Adding her support to the campaign for colored pilots in the armed forces, airminded Mrs. FDR on a recent tour to Tuskegee Institute was taken on an air tour of the spacious and beautiful campus at Tuskegee. . . . Showing not the slightest disdain, Mrs. Roosevelt trusted her life to the capable hands of a colored aviator, Chief Anderson. This is a splendid example of democracy in action."

We had been part of a successful attempt to break through the color barriers. By working within the legal structure, we had effected a change that would, ultimately, make a difference for all Americans. A new era in American history had begun, and we were jubilant; history was not only launched, but a brighter future for Negro Americans was endorsed and implemented by congressional appropriations.

CHAPTER THREE

ON OUR RETURN TRIP TO CHICAGO, DALE AND I were feted and feasted. A reception given by the National Airmen's Association was held for us on Chicago's Southside. And that night something more important to me than any other single event in my life occured. I met Anne Howard, the woman who was to become and remain my wife. She was beautiful, a sixteen-year-old girl dressed in a graceful pink dress with a large, broad-brimmed matching hat. She had come to the reception with her parents, her dad, Clyde Howard, who was as avid about flying as I was. It was he who had driven down to Sherwood, Ohio with Cornelius Coffey, licensed aircraft mechanic, to deliver a new crankshaft to Dale and me when we were downed at the beginning of our ten-city tour. Clyde Howard and I were acquaintances and mutual admirers of each other's flying aptitude, but his admiration did not extend to my interest in his young daughter.

His daughter, too, did not respond favorably that night to my overtures. When I asked her to dance, she told me she was too tired. That took me by surprise. After all, I was the guest of honor. I hadn't anticipated a rejection. Usually, most girls were impressed with me and "my line of jive." Because of a slight resemblance to Clark Gable, some called me Clark Gable Spencer, and because I was a flyer, there was also the usual element of hero-worship associated with the romantic image of the pilot. The *Chicago Defender* ran a weekly gossip column called "Everybody Goes When The Wagon Comes." It kept the city abreast of what I and other men-about-town were doing. My exploits and popular image with the girls were well-known to Anne Howard, but this didn't seem to impress her. The following Sunday, Anne and her parents came to the airport for their customary Sunday afternoon outing. I took the opportunity to seek her out. "Hi snooty puss," I greeted her. I was still abashed at her refusal to dance, but still intrigued by her easy dismissal of me. I had never met a girl who seemed to have such a strong image of herself; I couldn't unduly impress her with my customary antics and jive talk as I could with other girls. Gradually, over a period of weeks, we talked more, always under the watchful eye of her protective father. We'd find excuses to take a car ride with each other—we'd have to pick up an airplane part or check on someone else's plane. As long as it was on "business," Anne's father had no objections, although he was always leary of the twenty year age difference between Anne and myself.

To the two of us, though, it made no difference. Anne wasn't intimidated by my age, but part of that was because I acted much younger than I was. It wasn't until I left the Army, three years later, that I became more serious minded. Like many men before and after me, the Army had a maturing quality on me. It straightened up many a young, idealistic man who had never faced the rigors of a strict regimen.

One day while Anne and I were alone on one of our "business" calls, I told her to say "prunes." "Prunes" she said as I kissed her. Henceforth, our cloak of "business associates" was removed and we became more serious about each other. Although her father objected, we began dating regularly. Sometimes we'd go nightclubbing; we might hear Duke Ellington or Tommy Dorsey, a surprisingly inexpensive entertainment at that time. Sometimes, while Anne and I danced everyone would stop and circle around us, watching fascinatedly as we twirled about the floor doing a smooth waltz. Often, we'd go down to the pier and buy smoked fish and eat it there while dangling our feet in the lake. Anne never did appreciate the expensive meals we indulged ourselves in at Morris Restaurant—a place where I was well-known and where the girls would quickly cluster around. This was in 1939 and we were married in August of 1940. Like most of the things I did, even my marriage proposal was unconventional. The blustery day that I proposed to Anne, we were standing in six inches of snow on the corner of 47th Street and South Parkway in Chicago. "How about gettin' married, kid?" I asked. "Oh, come on. Quit it and be serious," she replied. She suspected I was pulling one of my fast moments of "jive," so I called a police officer over and asked him to witness the proposal. That convinced her and we became engaged.

When Anne's father saw the diamond ring I had bought her, he stormed to my apartment. When I answered the door, he blurted, "Here's the ring you gave Anne. I want you to take it back." He thrust it into my hand and I took it but it wasn't long before Anne had it back again and her father, though still reluctant, gradually succumbed and attended our wedding on August 18, 1940 at Chicago's Harlem Airport Clubhouse, a place where Anne and I had spent much time together. True to my flippant nature at the time, I was half an hour late to our wedding, having been delayed by the need to find a new best man, mine, Dale White, having caroused too much the previous night. Reverend Lewis, the same minister who had lectured me on self-discipline twenty years previously, performed the ceremony. Anne is still my wife today after thirty-three years of marriage, and her support has been extremely important to me over these years. As with any marriage, it took a little time to familiarize ourselves with each other's habits. Celebrating my first check from the Post Office, where I worked for a short time, I gave Anne the check telling her to buy herself a dress, not thinking that she would spend the entire amount of money. When she returned with a matching yellow dress, gloves, purse and lemon-shaped hat, I began to worry about our expenses for the week. Luckily, I was in a car pool and thus there was little expense for transportation. We charged the groceries that week. Anne explained, "I thought you meant for me to spend the whole check. Every September, my dad used to give me one of his checks so I could buy a complete new outfit. I guess I just didn't think."

It was near this time of my life that I was chosen, because of my style in the air shows, to test a new triangular form of parachute invented by Hoffman Company. The *Chicago News* recalled the incident this way:

> Last week, a crowd of thrilled spectators stood horror-stricken as Chauncey Spencer leaped from an aeroplane, flying at only 2,000 feet, and hurtled through the air at a speed of 176 feet per second for some 900 feet before opening the untried parachute which was his only hope for a safe landing.
>
> . . . All former tests with this chute have been performed with sand bags, dummies, etc.
>
> Because of the low altitude from which the daredevil jumped, it seemed sure death for him to wait more than a second or two to open the chute, but, as its value for short distance jumps was one of the claims being tested, Spencer waited a full ten seconds before pulling the cord.

What the newspaper didn't mention was that I had waited too long to pull the rip cord. Though I had one watchful eye on my altimeter during my descent, the other eye was on the crowd of spectators, including my cousin Roger Spencer and his friends who had come to see me make the jump and whom I wanted to impress. And I was more than a little aware of the cameras directed upwards at me. When I finally did pull the rip cord, it was too late. I felt the pull of my neck as it snapped upward. And so, rather ingloriously for a five-foot-ten-inch daredevil, I had to be carried off the field to a waiting ambulance. I was paralyzed, luckily enough, for only ten days.

Undaunted by that incident, I parachute jumped many more times. Often, the jumpers would purposely tantalize

39

the crowd of spectators. One stunt was to carry a sack of flour under our arms and as we jumped from the plane, we'd open the sack, leaving a trail of powdery smoke behind us as we descended through the air. This created quite a sensation with the pleased crowd.

My own special stunt was to parachute from the airplane and then unbuckle my harness and let my parachute float out into the sky. The crowd would see me falling, without the benefit of a chute, and go wild. I could hear their din as I descended several hundred feet above the ground. Then, at the last possible moment, I'd pull the rip cords to my second, partially-concealed parachute. The crowd, almost with synchronized precision, would breathe a single sigh of relief.

In March, 1941, hoping to later enter the now-integrated Air Corps, I enlisted in the Army and was stationed at Fort Custer in Battle Creek, Michigan.

My Army experience was a discouraging one to me. Along with thousands of other soldiers, I got a taste of the rigid caste system dividing officers and non-coms. One of my first negative experiences occurred at the Bellman's and Waiter's Club, where I had gone for a drink. Three officers came into the club and loudly ordered two privates to let them and their female guests have the table.

"We need this table. Now. Just leave your stuff here and get out." Without a word of rebuttal, the privates left.

I was so incensed by the incident, I later confronted one of the officers who said that, "Hell, they have to learn what an order is. It's as simple as that. These guys have got to learn how to take it."

"That's a bunch of bull. You're just throwing your weight around. You're not talking about how to take an order," I responded.

"Spencer, you're out of step. You don't know what it's all about. You could become an officer if you wanted to. Instead, you're worried about this kind of shit."

And I was concerned about the favoritism, the fact that no draftees were promoted, the blatant misuse of officers' powers. Low-ranking soldiers were ordered to clean officers' houses, to babysit for their children. Stiff penalties were incurred for soldiers' minor infractions. It was certainly not the kind of experience where one would learn to respect authority.

While I was in the Army, Anne lived with my parents in Lynchburg, Virginia. On her bus ride there she became a bit ill, for she was always subject to car sickness. A young white college student befriended her and periodically brought her glasses of water. His amazement was apparent when he later saw my wife, whose light-skinned complexion causes many people to think she's white, get off the bus and embrace my father, a dark-skinned Negro.

We've experienced many other incidents of amazement as people stared at us and then quickly averted their eyes when we glanced at them. Like my father, I'm dark-complected. One time, while my wife and I were standing on a street corner waiting to cross an intersection, a lady driver stared, unbelievingly, so long and hard at us that she rammed into the car in front of her. Admittedly, I thought some poetic justice had been achieved. It became my policy to grandly, with a slight bow, tip my hat to the incredulous gawkers.

And sometimes we couldn't help but invite the oh-so-incredulous, open-mouthed expression on the faces of people watching us. While riding the "L" in Chicago, Anne and I were frequently forced to sit apart because of lack of seats on the train. Often, I'd sit up front and Anne would sit in back. Glancing backwards, I'd make eyes at her. The white men, thinking I was flirting with a white woman, would become incensed. Anne had to save me just in time by coming and standing near me, letting others know that she knew me and that I was not bothering her.

Anne arrived at my parents' brightly-lit home in Lynchburg to the smell of freshly baked rolls and stewed oysters, a delicacy in Virginia. She was made very welcome, but found that dressing for dinner was not quite what she had expected. To eighteeen-year-old Anne, "dressing for dinner" meant wearing a nice dress, but to my mother it meant dressing formally, which my family frequently did. Upon seeing Anne's wardrobe, my mother invited Anne to the dress shop to look for a gown, but because Anne was a tiny size three, they had to shop in the children's section. She did find, however, an appropriate floor-length velvet skirt, suitable for my mother's rather elaborate preparations.

Anne liked Lynchburg, although some of the townspeople went out of their way to remind her that she was my second wife. Virginians were indeed class conscious and liked to marry their own, and, in particular, disliked Virginians marrying Northerners. But Anne gradually fit into the community, particularly through the efforts of my father, whom she regarded as an angel. Pop took particular care to chauffeur Anne around, to make sure she had extra spending money, to even escort her to the town dances.

Anne sent me a letter to Fort Custer shortly after her arrival in Lynchburg. "Liar," she wrote, "why did you tell me all those fibs?" Kidder that I was, I had made up stories about my hometown. Most Northerners were willing to believe the worst about the South and I played on their gullibility. I had told Anne that no Negroes were allowed downtown at night; that there was toilet water and sewage running under our house; that all the Negroes lived in a very muddy area with no grass around their houses. To emphasize the latter, I gave her a pair of galoshes as a going-away present. She believed the stories, and that was all I needed to exaggerate them.

Actually, adjoining our home is a beautiful flower garden tended by my mother. The smell of honeysuckle was pervasive there. As soon as mother, "Miss Anne," arrived home from her job as a librarian, she would head for the garden, stopping only long enough to pick up a tray of snacks already prepared for her. Often, she wouldn't come in until dusk. Either she was working with her flowers, which she cross-bred, or she'd be reading and writing in the garden house. This was my mother's world, the only world in which she felt comfortable. So my wife Anne took particular comfort in the attentions of my father and my Aunt Marietta.

After serving in the 184th Field Artillery Regiment, an all-Negro regiment, for eight months, I applied for appointment as a flying cadet in the first Negro Air Corps being formed that summer at Tuskegee, Alabama. Much to my disappointment, at age thirty-five, I learned that I had already exceeded the age limit for acceptance. I was released from active military service under the twenty-eight year age law in September, 1941.

Instead of going to Tuskegee, Anne and I went to Patterson Field in Fairfield, Ohio, where I qualified for a $1,620 per year job as an instrument repairman. Located a few miles from Dayton, the base served as a clearing house for all equipment used by the Air Corps. I was the first Negro to work in aircraft instruments with something besides a broom.

Many white employees were at first obviously bitter at my presence. Their resentment wasn't hidden. If I'd walk into the lavatory, the place would quickly empty. If I'd walk near the work bench, they'd walk away. From eight A.M. until five P.M., no one broached a conversation with me. I ignored it. One week later, my only friendly co-worker confided, "You're breaking the soul of these guys." I could see them subtly watching me while I quickly and efficiently repaired the auto-giro pilots. I was good at it and they couldn't help but notice and admire. Unable to contain their inquisitiveness, they soon began to ask how I could repair the instruments so fast, and gradually I won their respect. Resentment slowly died away in the eight months I worked there until June, 1942.

It is interesting to note here, that Executive Order 8802, issued by President Roosevelt, in 1941, was considered to be one of the biggest bluffs of the century. This bluff was spearheaded by the President of the Brotherhood of Sleeping Car Porters, A. Phillip Randolph. At that time Mr. Randolph had had quite a few talks with President Roosevelt urging that legislation be introduced to protect all Negroes and all other minority groups against discrimination because of race, color, national origin or creed, within all Federal agencies and industries having government contracts.

Mr. Randolph told the President that unless some Federal legislation was enacted, that he intended, with the help of the NAACP, the Urban League and many many other Negro organizations, to march on Washington and onto the White House lawn with 50,000 protestors. This was in the early stages of World War II. It was generally agreed at that time, among many Negro newspaper reporters and key Negro leaders, that Mr. Randolph could not have mustered up 500 marchers who would go to Washington because of their geographical location and their economic conditions.

Along with Mr. Randolph, Mary McLeod Bethune, an advisor to the President and working closely with Mrs. Eleanor Roosevelt, was also involved in this matter of marching. Mary McLeod Bethune was the head of Bethune College which later merged with Cookman Institute and became known as the Bethune-Cookman College.

It was May, 1941, and President Roosevelt's Executive Order 8802 had just become law, ruling out discrimination at Federal installations. After checking my records and background, Colonel Estabrook, Commanding Officer at Patterson, said I would be needed to work in Personnel and Administration to ensure compliance with the new Order. I was first sent by Judge William H. Hastie, the Civilian Aide of the Secretary of War and Colonel Estabrook, the Commanding Officer, Patterson Field to Tuskegee, Alabama, Tuskegee Army Air Force—Sub-Depot (TAAF-Sub-Depot) to work undercover, posing as an aircraft mechanic in order to study and report on the suspected and reported bad conditions there.

The situation there was even more deplorable than I had imagined it might be. The eating accommodations for Negroes were primitive. About two hundred Negroes were crammed into a room no bigger than twenty feet square where they sat on pop crates and ate from makeshift wooden tables. Mosquito nets were thrown over the food as they waited in line.

The whites had a spotless dining room with table linen and uniformed Negro waitresses to serve them. I was disgusted to see such a demonstration of racial prejudice, and yet I knew that this was typical not only for government installations but also for private industry throughout the nation.

The discrimination there was blatant. I had a government check which I attempted to cash at the bank; they refused.

I admired a pair of shoes in a store window and I went inside. "I'm interested in those black and white shoes in the window," I told the clerk. He immediately took them from the window and started wrapping them.

"I want to try them on first."

"You won't try them on in here," he replied.

"Well, then, I don't want them."

"Oh, yes, you *do* want them. I've already got them out. You're not going to come in here and start making trouble." The belligerence was unmistakable. His voice cut through the air and reflected a chilling stillness that had come over the room.

Recognizing trouble ahead, I paid for the shoes and left. To this day, I still have those shoes in my closet, dry-rotted and ill-fitting as they are—a reminder of those days to which there can be no return.

I was on the Tuskegee base less than three hours when a white supervisor came over to me and asked, "Is your name Spencer?" When I answered in the affirmative, he said, "You see that broom over there? I want you to get it and sweep up this hangar!" I refused, saying I was an instrument mechanic, not a janitor.

"I don't give a damn what you are," he said. "You're going to sweep up this hangar or go back north." But I didn't sweep and I didn't go north. Hopefully, those days were over. I hadn't heard the last of the incident, however.

The next day, the provost marshall, George Webb, a Negro, had me arrested and brought to his office. "What are you doing here? What's going on?" he demanded. His indignation was countered with equal force by my own. I told him I was an instrument repairman and insisted on knowing why he had had me arrested—a civilian and not under his jurisdiction—and if he had any charges to prefer

45

as a civilian to do so because I intended to clear the matter of his military arrest.

He said the Field Athletic Instructor at Tuskegee had told him that I was riding around in my car in the square flashing my bright lights in everyone's eyes. I denied the report but again asked what he had to do with the matter even if it were true. I was given a five day suspension with the corresponding loss of pay. This was later rescinded, of course, when my duties as an undercover agent were completed, but it became part of the documentary evidence of discrimination.

There was much more evidence, too. When I first arrived at Tuskegee, all the Negroes, about three hundred of us, were called together in an assembly. The white officer, Lt. William Williams from Boston, who was conducting the meeting called a few whites, all shop foremen, up to the front of the stage. He introduced them saying that "they are the law in here and what they say goes. I've found out that a Yankee has a hell of a time down here, so I'm going along with the tide. Now look, I'm a man from Boston. I know what this poverty and the situation is and I'm making a career out of this Army. I want all of you down here to realize you're in the South and you're going to do what the Southern white man wants you to do and I want you to get that through your thick skulls." No need to make it any plainer; we all got the message.

The city, too, was rampant with discrimination. The theater had two box offices; one labeled "colored," the other "whites."

One afternoon while driving down a nearly-deserted highway, my wife and I saw ahead of us a group of Klansmen, in white sheets and hoods, having a cross burning on the side of the road. "Hit the floor," I ordered my wife. Small as she is, she easily crawled down under the car dashboard. It wouldn't do at all to pass by the KKK with a white-looking woman in the car. Having no alternative, I passed by the ten-or-so hooded men who looked menacing in their white robes but they only stared at my car and let me pass by. It was my first encounter with the KKK and I would never want it repeated.

I sent my report on the very bad discriminatory conditions at Tuskegee to Colonel Estabrook and contacted Judge William H. Hastie, as I was instructed to do. Judge Hastie called me to say he was flying down to confer with me about the conditions that needed changes.

Several months later, the top command at Tuskegee Sub-Depot was changed and replaced with Lt. Colonel Noel Parrish as Commanding Officer. A new operation of policies was in force; hopefully, a new day was dawning in which all Americans would be treated as American citizens without regard to race. There was a long road ahead, but it was a step in the right direction.

CHAPTER FOUR

MY UNDERCOVER WORK AT TUSKEGEE HAVING been completed, Anne and I returned to Patterson Field in Fairfield, Ohio, 20 miles from Dayton, where my serious work in Personnel and Public Relations began. It wasn't long before I realized this was going to be the real test of my ability to cope with difficult situations.

In my job as Employee Relations Officer, could I make Executive Order 8802 work at Patterson Field, one of the larger air depots in the United States? A place where whites were not accustomed to having a Negro supervisor—a place where Negroes and other non-white employees were only in menial jobs and laborer positions. Some said there would be blood in the streets upon implementation of the integration order. Many whites claimed they would quit in protest if the orders were carried out.

I had many months of frustration and despair. As I made friends, I made enemies. Many Negroes wanted special favors. They expected that because I was a Negro, I would overlook their lack of qualifications, or their absences or their supervisor's reprimands. Some wanted to be immediately appointed aircraft mechanics, although they had no training in that field. Some wanted to operate expensive aircraft machinery, though their only experience had been as semi-skilled garage-shop mechanics. Many argued that because they were college graduates, they felt, even though they had, perhaps, majored in music or physical education or other unrelated training, they could quickly pick up the skill necessary to do work beyond their present knowledge.

My attitude differed. I'm an American first; a so-called Negro second. We had been asking for an opportunity. Now, here was a chance for economic security and an opportunity to get a decent job. I, too, was tired of going through school, going through college and coming out being a truck driver or a shoe-shine boy. On the other hand, on my travels through Appalachia going to Virginia, I often thought that there's nothing in this world that doesn't happen to all people, although Negroes did seem to be singled out for more than their share of prejudice. But I felt if we were going to accomplish our aims, we'd have to get respect as any other individual in this country. Nothing is to be gained if Negroes obtain employment merely because they are Negroes and not because they have gained necessary qualifications and respect. Without respect and training, it is mere tokenism, which robs Negroes or any other people of their dignity. We needed an opportunity, a chance to prove ourselves, no special favors.

My first week on the job, a Negro woman was sent to me. She had been suspended from her job for non-excused absence of several days. When she saw me, she immediately became indignant. "I don't want to talk to him. I want to talk to a white man." The whites were not the only ones on base with color prejudice. We ourselves, as Negroes, had inculcated the white man's attitude. Some Negroes' theme song was, "Who does that nigger think he is?" Many of us didn't respect ourselves; how, then was anyone else going to?

By both Negroes and whites, I was being called a Communist and an Uncle Tom, the choice epithets of the day. Many workers were suspicious, and there was a great deal of mistrust between management and employees that had to be removed. It was definitely going to take time.

And then, of course, there were those in authority in the Air Force who warned me not to do my job. They wanted integration in name only. Actually, they wanted to soft-pedal or even ignore it. I was warned explicitly to "drag my feet" on integration, and I was told to think the matter over carefully and remember that my esteem in the Air Force would be in exactly inverse proportion to the success of my accomplishment. I hadn't agreed to take this job in order to salve someone's conscience that the anti-segregation orders were being implemented. I told them that I intended to do my best to accomplish my assignment to implement FDR's order.

Here at Patterson, Negroes were for the first time given a great opportunity. The orders from Washington proscribed the practice of coding applications. Previously, a vain attempt was made to conceal coding by using numbers to indicate race on job application forms. Now, race could not be used as a reason for failing to hire a Negro.

In two years, the program was in full force. I worked closely with James C. Evans, an assistant to Judge Hastie, and Truman Gibson in the Secretary of War's Office. Of 18,000 workers, 3,000 were Negroes. Negros were functioning as research specialists, chemists, physicists, typists, clerks, printers and auditors. Many were supervisors of integrated units. Patterson Field had finally become a place where the majority of racial problems had been reduced to a minimum.

There were times when problems arose that were quickly settled. One case came when a white girl charged that a Negro employee was harassing her. A hearing board was formed to examine the charges and to decide on a course of action. I was chairman of the committee. After questioning the girl, we were unable to find any concrete acts of harassment by the defendant.

Finally I asked her, "What has this man actually done that has upset you so much?"

She replied, "Well, everytime I look up, he's looking at me!"

I said, "Don't you think this just might be flirtation, since he sees you looking at him?"

The case was ended at this point, and the man did not lose his job.

Cleveland's *Call Post* newspaper on December 23, 1944, reported a headline caption stating "Patterson Field is an integrated unit of skills with no place for the saboteur, Jim-Crow." The article read: "When one considers that four years ago, only Negro janitors were on the employee-roster of Patterson Field, and that today there are thousands of Negro civilians in all departments contributing to the expansion of the air forces of this country, only then can the full scope of Chauncey E. Spencer's heroic accomplishments be fully discerned. In 1940 there were twenty-three Negro janitors at Patterson Field. In 1944 there are six-hundred Negroes working in all capacities. When we asked his opinion of racial differences, Spencer replied studiedly, 'The only way to wipe out the race problem is to abolish the poll tax, amend states' rights, and have mixed schools everywhere.' "

Employees were working side by side in all departments —concerned about winning the war and unconcerned about segregation or social problems. By March, 1947, approximately nine thousand Negroes were employed in skilled and semi-skilled jobs at Wright-Patterson Air Force Base. Headlines in the *Pittsburgh Courier* on March 20, 1948 read: "Wright-Patterson Seen as Nation's Finest Experiment." Continuing it read: "All during the war, when problems of integration and fair employment practices were discussed, attention was called to the work being done in the field of race relations . . . at Wright-Patterson Field."

For my efforts, I received a decoration for exceptional civilian service from the Secretary of the Army. However, condemnation accompanied commendation. I was having problems with a newspaper publisher. A Negro-owned newspaper, the *Ohio State News*, published by Llewellyn "Jack" Coles, began publishing attacks against me. A series of articles which appeared in the paper from November, 1944 through February, 1945 referred to my having discriminated against members of my own race. An article entitled "Questions Chauncey Spencer Should Be Able To Answer Concerning Patterson Field" occurred in the paper on March 3, 1945. It read:

To the casual observer who visits the field, it is impossible not to be impressed with what you see. Negro men and women are working side by side at desks with white workers and complete integration into this particular war activity seems perfectly obvious. . . . Our quarrel with the set up was not directed at the lack of employment of colored persons. . . .

Are Negro employees given ratings on their experience and qualification alone? Are they upgraded on the same basis as are other workers?

Are regular channels as freely open to them as they are to other employees of Patterson Field? Are they discharged only after hearings and have they the right to appeal or does Chauncey Spencer have the power to separate colored employees from the federal payroll without a hearing as is prescribed in civil service procedures? Do other counsellors (white) have the same power over white employees as does Spencer?

Some Negroes at Patterson Field wanted to believe the innuendos; they wanted to believe that they were being mistreated. This made it doubly difficult for me. I was caught in the middle with pressure coming from both sides, Negro and white.

On January 13, 1945, the *Ohio State News,* published an editorial, "Let's Get Down to Brass Tacks" expressing concern for the Negro's business and economic problems, and next to it was a column attacking me called "The Inner Wheel" by Shad Jones.

Having read the diatribe, my mother was incensed. Her letter to the Editor was scorching:

Again this long spite crusade against my son would have gone its way with no word from me in his behalf. He is a man. He has been raised—raised is right—to tote his own weight; raised not with people in a house, but with parents in a home. You, and your henchmen actually seem to have a morbid talent for not letting bad enough alone. That is where I come in.

In your last release you reached back behind my son and dragged in his family. I suppose this is another one of your ways to help the Negro people! Yes, we are average American humans. Folk who work hard; avoid any special limelight when we can do so; respect others as we ourselves demand respect—something to glow about when save, for the Grace of God, we could be putrid. We pay our taxes, cast our ballot for our rights. We know, too, that rights and duties are the twins born to every true citizen. We like it that way.

This is a long letter, but not so long as the sum total of the attacks I now resent which your paper has unfairly made week after week. I hope your sixth sense will reveal the duty of a good newspaperman, and let you print this.

—Anne Spencer

My reputation being harmed both in the community and at Wright-Patterson, I decided to sue the newspaper. My wife, Anne, in her job at Wright-Patterson as Placement Officer, heard some of the gossip and innuendos made about me. Not knowing that Anne was my wife, a co-worker one day began talking about Chauncey Spencer's always being seen with a white woman. "You should see those two. I hear that they were holding hands once in broad daylight. Real bold. I wonder if his wife knows what's going on." A second co-worker quickly silenced her by saying that "that 'white woman' is his wife and she's standing right next to you."

Parts of this trial were near the absurd. The defense for the *Ohio State News* brought forth a witness who testified that I had discharged him illegally from Wright-Patterson. When asked in what year this incident occurred, the man replied, "1938." His testimony was, of course, thrown out since I had not been at Wright-Patterson until 1941.

Some of the reason behind the slanderous statements about me by the *Ohio State News* was feuding in the local branch of the NAACP. My position at Wright-Patterson was thought to be a powerful one, and leaders of the local NAACP were jealous, especially because I was an outsider. As usual with large organizations there was suspicion towards people from headquarters or from other branches. The local NAACP secretary had always wanted credit for our successful integration programs at Wright-Patterson.

More than nine months later, and after a four day trial and many witnesses, I won my lawsuit against the *Ohio State News* and was awarded $3,500 in damages. There was later an appeal by the defendant to the Court of Appeals for Franklin County, Ohio, but the original verdict was upheld.

A newspaper reporter for the *Pittsburgh Courier*, Al Dunmore, whom I had met in 1943 was sticking close by and assisting me with coverage and supporting me in my fight for integration and my reputation. He had covered the success story at Patterson Field and we had become close friends. Our lives had paralleled in many ways.

Al had always been interested in the involvement of Blacks in the Armed Forces. He, himself, first became aware of segregation when he was a company clerk enrolled in a segregated CCC Camp in 1936. He attempted to enlist in the Army and was told there was a quota system; the only vacancies for Blacks in the Armed Forces at that time were in the Ninth and Tenth Cavalry, and portions of them were located at West Point where they were used as stable hands.

During the Dayton days, Al and I worked very closely on a special assignment for James C. Evans who was then top aide to the Secretary of Defense. We were to study the segregation at Lockbourne Air Force Base in Columbus, Ohio. My assignment to implement the integration orders covered all of the Air Force bases, not only Patterson Field. It was in that capacity that I was asked to study the specific integration problem at Lockbourne.

We began to realize that as long as there was an all-Negro Air Corps, then stationed at Lockbourne, there would always be a bottleneck in the upward movement of the Negroes. Here at Lockbourne, where most top-rated Negroes were attracted to the 332nd Fighter Group, there was an abundance of Negro talent. We encouraged the men to request transfers, integrate, spread out some of that talent. But they balked; they were happy the way they were, separate as they were, and basically unconcerned about what the larger issue of a "separate but equal" Black Air Corps meant for future generations of Negroes. This was their playhouse; they didn't have to compete with the "fay boys," their jargon for whites. One of the reasons for their reluctance from the officer's point of view was the fact that they feared the competition through integration would cause their separation from the military and their loss of jobs. They feared returning to civilian life where they would have to pound the streets looking for jobs and face discrimination in employment. Here at Lockbourne, they had good jobs. It was a known quantity to them and they didn't have to fight for their rights.

Also stationed at Lockbourne were the 99th and 100th Pursuit Squadrons under the command of General Benjamin O. Davis, Jr., first Negro General of the U.S. Air Force. Brigadier General B. O. Davis, Jr., was a West Point man who had undergone the silent treatment during his cadet years. When Al Dunmore and I were at Lockbourne trying to implement the President's orders for integration of the armed services we talked to some of Davis's staff men. The story was the same; these pilots did not want to compete with all-white squadrons and possibly end up being separated from the service.

Their fear and suspicion were so great that when word got out that Al and I were investigating, we were put under military arrest. Within a matter of hours our official status was confirmed by Washington and we were released. It should have been evident that mandatory integration would go into effect no matter what some people wanted or were afraid of.

Their fears were understandable. However, the inevitable followed. The President's Executive Order directing integration was assigned to Mr. James Evans to implement and he directed Al Dunmore and I to ferret out the opposition. The Lockbourne Air Force Base was eventually integrated and without all the terrible predictions of disaster manifesting themselves.

When it was known integration was to become effective,

however, certain officers at Lockbourne Base realized that there was between thirty to forty thousand dollars in the Officer's Club Fund and they made plans to appropriate it for their own use rather than turn it over to its proper office. Six staff officers called a reporter, Billy Rowe, with the *Pittsburgh Courier* and outlined a plan by which they would use his services to act as a go-between in setting up a gala week of expensive entertainment, such as scheduling big band entertainment with Duke Ellington and Lionel Hampton, or staging shows and banquets. If the fee was two thousand dollars, the reporter would pad the fee to show it to be four or six thousand dollars. The reporter would earn a thousand dollars and turn the remainder over to the six officers. Through this means the officers could turn in ten thousand dollars and split the padded amount among themselves. The plan backfired on them as soon as the *Courier* reporter was given all the details. He reported their proposition to the Editor-in-Chief, and the matter was stopped. The money was turned in to the proper office in Washington, D.C. and thus a scandal was aborted at the beginning of the Air Force integration program.

Having had success thus far, my job expanded to raise base morale and consequent work output. I was placed in charge of staging basewide entertainment shows and promoting favorable camp-community relations. A greater and greater percentage of the really important part of my work took place evenings in my home.

In 1943, my wife and I decided to build a home in Dayton. We paid the deposit fee on the land we chose in hopes of building a brick, ranch type home there. We signed the agreement-to-purchase papers. Making definite plans to build there, Anne and my father, who happened to be visiting us, went to the new land to check on fence measurements. It didn't take long for the white neighbors to spot my dark-skinned father and neither did it take them long to notify the land's owner who was in Florida. Upon hearing that we were Negro, she immediately rescinded the deal. We decided not to fight the case, and so found another house in a different section of Dayton.

We lived in this white, cottage-type house with a weeping willow tree in front and a guest house in back until 1956. Beautiful shrubbery and a grape arbor made it a very comfortable home. It was an ample home, as, indeed, it had to be for our purposes. Many Negroes who came to Wright-Patterson on official business trips could not find hotel accommodations and, thus, stayed at our home. We always had extra guests there, sometimes two or three at one time.

The constant entertaining my wife and I indulged in as part of my expanded job was depleting my salary at a greater rate than my steady but small promotion could compensate for. In desperation, my wife and I looked about for an added source of income. In February, 1951, we began operating a drive-in restaurant, a Park-Mor Drive In. To the best of my knowledge, it was one of the first drive-in restaurants of its kind in the Dayton area with integrated personnel. In my job capacity of implementing then Executive Orders 9980-9981, I was out of town a great deal visiting other government installations. My wife, besides holding down her full-time job at Wright-Patterson, and being a mother to our children, actually ran the restaurant. She hired and fired, did all the ordering and bookwork, and even filled in as cook when necessary. By dint of hard work, long hours and herculean exertions on Anne's part, the enterprise was turned into a money-maker. Thanks to this added income we were able to continue the entertainment that was a necessary part of my work and save some money in addition. Were it not for this restaurant business and the savings therefrom, I would not have had sufficient funds to begin to fight the charges which were later brought against me. In the meantime, though, things were going well.

In January, 1948, I was awarded the highest honor the Air Force can bestow upon a civilian, the Exceptional Civilian Service Award. The Certificate accompanying the award reads:

Exceptional Civilian Service Medal

For exceptional service with the Army Air Force at Wright Field during World War II. His outstanding achievements in racial relations at headquarters, Air Materiel Command, his contributions in establishment of public good will, and his tireless and conscientious employee relations have won the respect of both employees and management and have been of invaluable assistance in accomplishing the mission of the Army Air Force.

This was only the calm before the storm. Nine months later, the storm raged in all its fury.

CHAPTER FIVE

I HAD REACHED THE TOP STEP OF A GS-11 IN SEP-tember, 1953, and my papers were being processed to become a GS-13, when out of a cloudless blue sky, lightning struck! Returning from a brief vacation in Philadelphia, I was handed a "Notice of Suspension" as a security risk. I was dumbfounded. The Air Materiel Command Personnel Office was as shocked as I to learn of the suspension and the charges brought against me. The charges had come down from Headquarters United States Air Force. At the time, I was assigned to the Inspector General's Office as an Employee Relations Officer. Prior to that, I had been the Chairman and Alternate Chairman of the Grievance Review Hearing Committee, Civilian Personnel Division HQ. AMC., worldwide.

Why credence was placed in these completely unfounded charges of my being a security risk is not totally a mystery, however. At the time President Truman's Executive Orders 9980 and 9981, ruling out discrimination specifically in the civilian and military, were promulgated, there were many highly-placed USAF Personnel Officials who did not wish to see this order effectively implemented. This was an early version of anti-integration sentiment in Civil Service.

Early in my career as Employee Relations Officer, I had been approached by John A. Watts, Headquarters USAF,

Director of Personnel, Washington, D.C., urging me to proceed slowly "and drag my feet" on integration. I had disregarded his admonitions. Now, apparently, I was reaping the effects of my zealous work.

Then, too, character assassination of government officials was not uncommon in 1953. It was the senator Joseph McCarthy, Roy Cohen and Dave Schine era; thousands of government jobs were going begging because of the rampant unfounded charges occurring in government circles. Often, unknown to each other, spies were spying on spies. "Black Lists" and false charges were appearing on many hundreds of American writers, military and government officials, lawyers, and citizens in all walks of life—all listed as "security risks" by over-zealous governmental agents. Espionage became the government's official modus operandi.

McCarthy was rarely able to prove his charges of government and military officials being card-carrying Communists. In the end, he did a tremendous disservice to our government by not only creating an atmosphere of suspicion and fear, but also by doing damage to the cause of anti-Communism. In 1954, the Senate finally censured him with a vote of condemnation.

In spite of the rampant spying that I knew existed, it came as a total shock to me to be considered a security risk. The highest Air Force personnel were obviously out to discredit me but, admittedly, neither did I have the full support of the workers at Wright-Patterson Air Force Base.

I would have to admit that I was not popular with some Negroes at the base. They resented the power, played up by the *Ohio State News*, that they thought I possessed. Some Negroes thought I had the power to say, "You eat; you sleep; you die; you go." That was not the case. But if they didn't do their job, they *would* go as far as I was concerned. I wouldn't play favorites, much to the chagrin of some Negro as well as white employees.

With hindsight, some of the reasons for the belief in the charges are apparent to me now. At the time the charges were brought against me, I was too shocked to think clearly.

When I told Anne about the charges, she thought I was joking.

The most frightening aspect of the entire affair was the total surprise of the charges. One month I had been awarded the Air Force's highest civilian honor. I maintained excellent working relations with my supervisors (as sworn testimony will show). And only a few months later I had my livelihood, my social standing, and my credit rating seriously threatened by those nineteen charges, any one of which, if proven true, could be the cause of my permanent discharge. Though the charges were yet unproven, I was, in reality, branded, and in the interim I was treated as if I were guilty. A presumption of innocence I definitely did not have.

A portion of that fatal letter and all of the charges brought against me read:

23 September 1953

Dear Mr. Spencer:

Reference is made to Air Force Regulation 40-12, dated 13 January 1950, which sets forth the principles and procedures governing the Air Force Loyalty-Security Program. A copy of Air Force Regulation 40-12 is attached. Investigation conducted pursuant to this regulation reflects information which, in the opinion of the Central Loyalty-Security Board, Headquarters, United States Air Force, raises a substantial doubt as to whether your continued employment with the Department does not constitute an unwarranted security risk. Accordingly, the Board has determined to initiate proceedings against you under Air Force Regulation 40-12 with a view toward effecting your removal from employment with the department . . .

The Central Loyalty Security Board's decision to initiate against you is based upon the following information:

1. During 1940 and thereafter, at Dayton, Ohio and elsewhere, you demonstrated a consistent lack of reliability as evidenced by numerous false official statements, deliberate misrepresentations, and frequent violation of laws and regulations as follows:

61

A. On a Civil Service Commission Personnel Information sheet, (Form 346A, July 1940) dated December 1940, you claimed to have attended Aeronautical University, Chicago, Illinois, from March, 1936 to June 1938, which was false.

(What had really happened, of course, was that I was given credit by Aeronautical University for training received from the Coffey School of Aeronautics.)

B. In a sworn Civil Service form, No. 375, executed 16 April 1942, you stated under oath that you had received 472 semester hours credit from Aeronautical University, Chicago, Illinois from March, 1936 to June 1939, which was false.

C. In an application for Federal Employment dated 27 May 1943, you claimed to have attended Aeronautical University, Chicago, Illinois, from March 1936 to June 1939 with 472.5 semester hours credit, claimed graduate work in Social Science, Mathematics and Chemistry, and claimed to have been a licensed pilot and licensed motion picture projectionist, all of which was false.

(Of course, I had a student's pilot license and had done a great deal of flying beyond what that particular license would allow. I had been a licensed motion picture projectionist in Lynchburg, Virginia when I had managed the Harrison Theatre in 1932 and 1933. My studies beyond the undergraduate level were all done on my own, not in an academic institution.)

D. In signed forms submitted to you in connection with Civil Service promotions, dated 16 May 1946 and 10 June 1948, you claimed attendance at Aeronautical University, Chicago, Illinois with 472.5 semester hours credit, which was false.

E. On or about 11 March 1949, you submitted a notice of injury in the men's room at Wright-Patterson Field, Dayton, Ohio, which was false.

(An insignificant injury, which happened to be true, however.)

F. On or about 2 November 1948 and at other times you "punched" time cards for other employees without authority to do so.

(I deny that I have ever punched time cards for any other employee other than myself and those few people who in later court testimony claimed that I did punch others' cards did perjure themselves.)

2. At Dayton, Ohio, in 1948 and early 1949, you wilfully and without authority disclosed classified information by revealing to Mrs. Will Griffin the existence of an Office of Special Investigations file and certain information pertaining to her therein contained.

3. On March, 1950, at Dayton, Ohio you admitted that while in Chicago, Illinois, you had been employed as a female impersonator and as a "bootlegger."

(The only time I was a bootlegger was when I helped secure liquor as a bell hop at seventeen years of age. I was a female impersonator, not in Chicago but in New York for three weeks. And as my attorney later pointed out, "We deny that this portrayal was in any manner whatsoever homosexual or perverted. No more than a chorus line in the 'This is the Army' show seen by me and countless members of soldiers in World War Two.")

4. In about August, 1950 at Peekskill, New York, you attended a Communist Party Rally featuring, among others, Paul Robeson. The Communist Party has been designated by the Attorney General of the United States as communist, subversive, and seeking to alter the form of government of the United States by unconstitutional means . . .

(On a trip to New York to attend my brother-in-law's funeral, I had, indeed, attended a rally featuring Paul Robeson.)

Upon receiving this letter, I was dismissed from my job until my court case could be heard. At first, I decided not to fight the charges; they were so extreme, so lacking in substance that I couldn't help but feel bitter. After all, I was supposed to be innocent until proven guilty. To fight the case meant I had to prove my own innocence. Realizing that our minds wouldn't rest until I was exonerated of the charges, my wife Anne urged me to clear my record, to bring the case to trial, and I ultimately decided to do just that.

The weeks before, during and after my trial are still like a bad nightmare. For nine months, from September, 1953, until I was completely exonerated in June, 1954, our family suffered harassment.

My eleven-year-old son was tormented and bullied at school. "Your father's an Uncle Tom." "Your mother and father like the people in Russia." "Your father doesn't like us colored people." These were the gibes children hurled at my son as they reflected what they had heard from their parents. Few neighbors would permit my son to play in their yards with their children.

I can recall waking in the night and hearing both my wife and son crying. At all hours of the day and night, even at three and four in the morning, the phone would ring. When the receiver was lifted—silence, nothing but silence. Subjection to harassment became a way of life for us. While walking up to the grocery store, Anne would not be welcomed for a ride in the neighbors' cars, as was customary before the security charges were brought against me.

People drove by and threw garbage on our lawn. During the Air Force's investigations, the Office of Special Investigation asked some of both our near and distant acquaintances what they knew of my "communistic leanings, bootlegging activities, and homosexual activities." One friend told us later that an investigator asked him if he had ever seen me in women's clothes. "Wasn't that a crazy thing to ask?" he questioned incredulously. Friends and even some relatives began to shy away from us.

With these clouds over my head, I was unable to obtain any other type of employment. I was even refused a job as

Chauncey's mother
Anne B. Spencer

Parents
Mr. and Mrs. Edward D. Spencer
Lynchburg, Virginia, 1938

Chauncey E. Spencer
5 years old
1911

Chauncey's birthplace, Lynchburg, Virginia, 1942

Childhood and Family

Chauncey
and Family
San Bernardino,
California
1962

Spencer's Immediate
Family, Front
Row: Chauncey I,
Kyle 12, Anne, Second
Row: Shaun 14, Carol 25,
Lu Juan 20, Third Row:
Edward 32, Chauncey II 19,
Joel 17, Michael 21.
Highland Park, Michigan
May 18, 1975

Chauncey and Tilly
January 1966
Home study with helper

Chauncey and Anne
with son, Edward II
and pet, Herr Vonn
Dayton, Ohio
1950

Dr. H. W. "Swipe" Reid
Reid Pharmacy
Lynchburg, Virginia

Pilot Chauncey E. Spencer
Age 31
Chicago, Illinois, 1937

Aviation Experiences

Chauncey (top right) with family and friends at National Airmen's Association Conference in Chicago, Illinois, 1939.

Left to Right: Representative from the noted Jones Brothers, (unidentified), Corneilius R. Coffey, President of National Airmen's Association, 1938; and Horace C. Kayton (far right) greet Dale L. White and Chauncey on their return to Chicago after their National Goodwill flight to Washington, May 18, 1939.

Chauncey, Mother Anne,
Dale White at
Preston Glenn Airport,
Lynchburg, Virigina
1939

(Above) Negro fliers who attended the First National Airmen's Association Conference in Chicago, Illinois, 1930. (Below) Chauncey, rival jumper, Willa Brown Chappel (contestant how highest licensed woman flight instructor rating) and friends at exhibition parachute jumps given to raise money and interest for Goodwill Flight to Washington, D. C. Harlem Airport, Chicago.

Chauncey and Dale greeted by Enoch P. Waters (embracing pilots), Editor of the Chicago Defender, and friends upon their return to Chicago from Washington after meeting with the Congressional Committee for appropriation to include Negroes into the Air Corps, 1939.

INTREPID CHICAGO AVIATORS PILOT 'OLD FAITHFUL' IN CROSS COUNTRY GOODWILL TO

Chauncey "Clark Gable" Spencer, left, and Dale White, Chicago aviators and representatives of the National Airmen's Association, with the airplane "Old Faithful", which they are piloting to eastern cities in behalf of the Air Show to be held in Chicago in August. From Pittsburgh where they arrived Friday, they flew to New York, landing Saturday morning. In Washington they will be greeted by several members of Congress and by Edgar G. Brown, valiant crusader for racial rights, who has conducted a successful flight for recognition of the Negro aviator in the Nation's law.

—Photo by Taylor

Dale L. White
Chauncey's friend
and copilot
Chicago, 1937

Tuskegee A A F
Training Command
briefing, 1943.

(Below) 332nd Contingent at Selfridge Air Force Base prior to overseas duty, 1943.

N. A. A. DEFENDER FLYERS WELCOMED HOME AFTER 3,000-MILE TOUR

Left Photo: Senator James Slattery (Dem. Illinois), receives congratulations from Dale L. White and Chauncey Spencer in his senate suit, Washington, D. C. May 15, 1939 for carrying on as successor to the James Hamilton Lewis, who championed move for training Race in $300,000,000 National Defense Act. Shown are, Left, to Right, Spencer, Senator Slattery, White and Edgar G. Brown, President of the United Government Employees, Inc. and Washington representatives of the National Airmen's Association of which White is vice president. Ben Hale and Cornelius Coffey, President of the N. A. A. are inspecting the broken shaft in center photo which forced the flyers down at Sherwood, Ohio, on May 10. While in Washington, White and Spencer dropped in on Congressman Everett McKinley Dirksen (Rep. III.). Dirksen introduced the amendment to the Civil Aeronautics Bill in the House of Representatives prohibiting discrimination on account of Race, Creed or Color in administration of the benefits of the Act. Left to Right: White, Congressman Dirksen, Floyd J. Smith, Washington pilot, Brown and Spencer.

Photos by McNeil and Murphy.

With the hope to set up colored aviation clubs all over the country, believing that such a movement will stimulate government appropriations much quicker, two pilots, representing the National Aviation Association of Chicago, visited the capitol on Monday and conferred with several officals, including Rep. Emmett O'Neil (Dem. Ky.), center, shown shaking the hand of Pilot Chauncey Spencer. Others in the group are, left to right: D. T. White, pilot and vice-president of the N. A. A. James W. Douglas, Business Manager of the Washington Pilots' Association and Edgar G. Brown, President of the United Government Employees.

Dale White and Chauncey Spencer, Chicago aviators, are greeted by Robert L. Vann, editor of the Courier, upon the occasion of their arrival in Pittsburgh from Cleveland. Left to Right: Chauncey Spencer, Dale White, Lieut. Jimmie Peck, Pittsburgh airman, and Mr. Vann. The editor of the Courier has shown a pioneer interest in aviation and a chance for Negro aviators. The Pittsburgh Courier, under his direction, initiated and promoted the flight to force Congress to recognize black flyers.

—Photo by John G. Taylor.

Adding her support to the campaign for colored pilots in the armed air services, air-minded Mrs. Franklin D. Roosevelt, on a recent visit to Tuskegee Institute, was taken on an air tour of the spacious and beautiful campus at Tuskegee by Albert Anderson, instructor of flying classes at the Alabama school. Showing not the slightest disdain, Mrs. Roosevelt trusted her life to the capable hands of a colored aviator. This is a splendid example of democracy in action.

Airplane View of
A. and I. State College
Nashville, Tennessee

World's Heavyweight
Champion Joe Louis
is shown in New York
with Chauncey Spencer,
left and Dale L. White,
right, fliers who were
guests of honor along
with the Champion at
a party at the Mino
Club in Harlem. The
affair marked the twenty-
fifth birthday of the Champion and the arrival in New
York of the fliers who
are nearing the end of a
3,000 mile air tour.

Left to Right: Flight Instructor, Spanky Roberts, B. O. Davis, Jr., Charles De Bow, Mac Ross, and Samuel Custis. The first five cadets who graduated from Tuskegee Air Base to become commissioned officers and pilots in the United States Air Force, 1942

A hearty welcome awaited flyers, Dale L. White and Chauncey E. Spencer on their arrival at Harlem airport, Chicago, Thursday afternoon completing a 3,000 mile good-will flight sponsored jointly by the National Airmen's Association and the Chicago Defender. Shown left to right: James Hill, manager, Jones Brothers Ben Franklin store; Cornelius R. Coffey, President of the N. A. A. White, Spencer and Horace Cayton, sociologist.
—Gushiniere Photo.

Although Negro aviators have fought and distinguished themselves in faraway lands and a black man was in charge of the air defense of Paris during World War, the military leaders of the United States ignore the intrepid black men who would serve their country in the air. The above pictures show only three of scores of young colored men who are ignoring prejudice and, at the greatest sacrifice and risk, attempting to equip themselves for service to their country. Dale L. White and Chauncey Spencer, members of the National Airmen's Association of Chicago, are making a city-to-city flight to interest Negro aviators in an Air Show to be held in Chicago in August and to place before the public the aspirations of the Negro aviator. In the center above, White and Spencer are shown as they arrived at the Allegheny County Airport, Pittsburgh, from Cleveland. At the left is Lieut. Jimmie Peck, Pittsburgh aviator, who distinguished himself on the side of the Loyalists in the Spanish Civil War and at the right, Spencer is shown getting "contact" for the flight from Pittsburgh to New York. Saturday morning, the flyers were greeted, as shown center, by Mrs. Bill "Bojangles" Robinson, wife of the famous tap-dancer and unofficial mayor of Harlem.

—Photos by John G. Taylor, Pittsburgh, and Bill Rowe, New York.

Civil Servant and Job Experiences

(Above) Chauncey participating in a program honoring the Air Force at Central State College (Wilberforce University) at Xenia, Ohio, 1945. (Left to Right) School's ROTC Director; Carl Jenkins of National Airmen's Association, Dr. Charles Wesley, University President; Al Dunmore, Pittsburgh Courier, James C. Evans, Airmen's Association. (Below) Award of the Exceptional Civilian Service Medal to Chauncey E. Spencer at Wright Field, Dayton, Ohio, January 23, 1948. (Left to Right) Colonel C. H. Welch, Public Information Officer, A. M. C.; Chauncey Major General C. B. Stone, Director, Supervision and Maintenance, A. M. C., Mrs. Edward Spencer, and wife Ann Spencer.

Chauncey in position of Civilian Personnel
Employee Relations Officer at Wright-
Patterson AFB, Ohio, 1947

a thirty-one-dollar-a-week janitor. The employer told me to come back "when this thing is cleared up." My salary, which had been $6,400 a year dwindled to a mere $187, the total sum I earned in my nine month suspension. Although Anne continued to work, money was becoming scarce. We were forced to give up our restaurant business. We re-mortgaged our home to feed our four children.

Often times I found it difficult to find the money to purchase milk for my infant son. Although I sometimes wanted to give up on the whole thing, Anne persistently urged me to fight it out. It was her support and determination that kept me from simply moving away, forgetting the entire mess, and trying to start over again.

During my period of unemployment, I started asking neighbors if I could paint their houses—free of charge—just to have something to do. I painted four houses during my enforced layoff.

I hired the law firm of Connelly, Cummings, and Kessler to defend me. The lawyers traveled to several cities to gather depositions. It was necessary to gather background material and character testimonials that would bury the charges forever. Overall, the cost of my defense was almost eighteen thousand dollars. Up until the time of the hearing, it cost us approximately eleven thosuand dollars for research, certifications, counter investigations and legal services. I would never have begun the proceedings if I knew how exorbitant the cost was going to be. All of our savings, the money from the forced closing of our business operation, and all I could borrow from friends and family were eaten up—to defend myself. I used every cent I could raise—including savings from my father—to defend myself. The Air Force, too, spent well over twenty thousand dollars in their attempt to discredit me.

The hearing was held, three months after my initial notification of suspension at Wright-Patterson Air Force Base on the 16th and 17th of December, 1953. A three-panel board was both the judge and jury.

At our initial appearance before the board, we were told by Agent Jennings that I alone could defend myself. My attorney, Carl D. Kessler (who is now Senior Judge for the City of Dayton), was allowed to be present and to advise me, but he could not question witnesses or defend me verbally. This injustice was never reversed, and as Colonel Andrew Meulenberg later testified, this was part of the attempt by the Office of Special Investigation to build up a case against me to report to USAF Headquarters.

Probably the most important single document which led to my clearance was a statement by a gentleman of unimpeachable character who placed his career in jeopardy by speaking out for me, Colonel Andrew Meulenberg, USAF Deputy Inspector General for Air Materiel Command and also Fair Employment Practices Officer for the Command during the period of my job incumbency. In his sworn statement, he said:

"I believe it was during the month of January or early February of 1951 that I was visited by agents of the Office of Special Investigation. These agents were investigating certain allegations against Mr. Chauncey Spencer and interviewed me because I was in a position of having frequent contact with Mr. Spencer. I do not remember the details of the allegations against Mr. Spencer nor do I remember the names of the agents who visited me. In my capacity as Deputy Inspector General I had frequent contact with OSI; these frequent contacts caused this particular visit to be extremely informal. I recall distinctly having a most unfavorable impression of the efforts of the investigators to spend their time on what appeared to me to be picayunish allegations made by people of very low professional and social standing. It was apparent to me that Mr. Spencer's enemies were hard at work trying to discredit Mr. Spencer's character and standing in the community. I also distinctly remember having the impression that the OSI agents were encouraging the submission to them of reports detrimental to Mr. Spencer, and these agents were actually looking for an opportunity to build up a sufficient file against Mr. Spencer so that action could be taken to discredit Mr. Spencer and have him removed from the Federal payroll.

I repeat that this statement is not intended to be critical

of the Air Force Security System and Loyalty Program. As a result of my one year's association with Mr. Spencer, I have the highest regard for him as an individual and the utmost faith in him as a loyal American citizen. Unless I am proven to be wrong, I maintain the world would be better off and that the colored race would be advanced a thousand times faster if it had a few more representatives like Chauncey E. Spencer."

Sworn character references by highly placed government officials were very necessary in my defense. Without them, I wouldn't have been cleared. But I also needed to factually defend myself against the plethora of misinformation and purposely contrived innuendos set forth by the prosecuting attorneys. One of the charges was that I was a female impersonator in Chicago. The prosecution attempted to insinuate that I was a sexual deviant. The transcript of my defense to the charge follows:

Mr. Spencer: I told him (Mr. Morill, OSI agent) that during high school we put on plays and I had been a female impersonator. I had done the thing so well when I went into college it came up; as a matter of fact, I remember in college we had a mock marriage and every participant in the mock marriage was a male. I was dressed as a female. Well, then, we had certain plays, all male plays. I saw one the other night, by the way, on television. The Triangle Club at Princeton. And do you mean to tell me these men because of participating in this particular show, what they were doing, will stop them from being our leaders, or our businessmen of the world, they're supposed to be involved in some perversion or homosexuality because of that: No. And I resent his statement.

Mrs. Zubrod: (Member of the Board hearing my case) I don't think that question was raised as Mr. Morrill's statement, but it did, I recall, say that you made money as a female impersonator. That's what I got from it. The money from it.

83

Mr. Spencer: I have never made money as an impersonator. After I left college I went to New York; jobs were hard to get and I thought I had an opportunity to go on the stage as a female impersonator. That lasted about three weeks because my sister told me my mother and father were coming to New York on a vacation and my stage career ended right then and there.

Mrs. Zubrod: Can you tell me the theatre and stage?

Mr. Spencer: Yes. It was the Lafayette Theatre.

Mrs. Zubrod: And that is where?

Mr. Spencer: In Harlem in New York City.

Mrs. Zubrod: Is that a legitimate theatre?

Mr. Spencer: Yes, it is. It's a legitimate theatre, very legitimate theatre. Some of our top performers started there. You could say that, as far as Negroes are concerned, to say that you were on the stage of the Alhambra or the Lafayette Theatre of New York would be similar to saying that you started at the top theatre, some big circuit on the white side in the entertainment world. That's what I'm trying to say.

Mrs. Zubrod: What kind of impersonations were those?

Mr. Spencer: It was a comedy impersonation. In one particular skit there were two dancers. I was a very good dancer. They did a burlesque of a scene from Romeo and Juliet in which I dressed up in a dress, and I was up on a balcony and as the spot light came on me, I had the black face and a long tress of blonde hair and he did this thing "Oh, Juliet," and so forth and so on to get the laughs.

Mrs. Zubrod: Was this all in New York, Mr. Spencer?

Mr. Spencer: Yes, it was. It was in New York.

Mr. Kessler: (My Attorney) Did you, at any time, ever either now, I want you to think carefully here, either for money or in some kind of a charity skit or any kind of a formal or informal presentation, were you ever a female impersonator in Chicago?

Mr. Spencer: No. I have never been. That was the end of my female impersonations.

Mr. Kessler: That ended it?

Mr. Spencer: When my sister said mother and dad are coming into New York, naturally, they looked upon this type of stage acting itself as being unacceptable. That was the end of my stage career there.

Mr. Kessler: Could you locate that as to approximately the year?

Mr. Spencer: I would say . . . it must have been about '26 or '27 I think.

This type of questioning played a major role at the hearing. On the same line, I was asked by John B. Collins, Attorney Advisor, Office of the Secretary of the Air Force, "I understand you are known to be quite a ladies' man, particularly with ladies of the white race. Isn't this true?"

I answered, "In my position I have contact with quite a few people of all races. However, if you questioned any women that I have worked with or been friendly with, of either the white or Negro race, I can assure you, you will not find one who will say that I have ever been less than a gentleman with any of them."

The prosecution left no stone unturned. No part of my private life was uninvestigated. They raked and fished through the past searching for character slips. "Bootlegger" was the term they tried to pin on me because as a seventeen-year-old bell hop, I had secured liquor for hotel customers. I was grateful to Colonel Meulenberg and the testimony he gave which stressed that the Office of Special Investigation appeared to be purposely trying to discredit me. They had an ax to grind and were grinding it for all they were worth. Luckily, I could scrape together enough money to defend myself. Others, I know, were not as fortunate as I and were ruined in the McCarthy era.

Another sworn statement by Colonel Ralph D. Penland, U.S.A.F. retired, shows clearly the unfounded basis for the charges brought against me. He offered this defense in my behalf: "Mr. Spencer worked directly under my office and supervision. I have personal knowledge that many of his assignments were given because the Comanding Generals placed great confidence in Mr. Spencer's qualifications, abilities and overall knowledge of his work.

"Shortly after Mr. Spencer came on the Base, as a result of an erroneous report, impersonating an officer, USAAC, my office and the Base Security Officer sent out inquiries and ran background check as to his character, integrity and training which resulted in no derogatory information being established against him. However, the inquiry was carried a step further, there were several reasons involved, but one in particular was that he was the first Negro to be assigned to Air-Craft Instrument Department and several white employees had openly stated their objections to his being placed in the Department. Mr. Spencer was given an oral and written examination in instrument work and he qualified far above the average, so much so, that though he was originally to have been assigned as a General Mechanic's Helper, he instead, was placed in an available position in the same Department as a Junior Instrument Mechanic. Being of the high calibre and type individual that he is, he immediately was in command of the friction elements. It was interesting to see the transformation of the employees who objected to his initial assignment within the Department later become very friendly and fond of him. He was closely observed and favorable reports continued to come to my attention and the Commanding General, M. G. Estabrook, through the Base Security Officer. When Executive Order 8802 became a part of the United States Army Air Corps policy, Mr. Spencer was selected by the Commanding General to monitor the programs. He objected, stating that due to certain racial opinions and attitudes, his monitoring of the program would place him in a cross-fire position wherein he would create enemies on both sides, white and Negro alike. General Estabrook assured him that he would have his entire staff's backing and cooperation to effectuate the program. Mr. Spencer agreed and was immediately transferred from Instrument Repair Department, after serving approximately nine months, to my office, Civilian Personnel. He did a remarkable, although at times it must have appeared to him as seemingly thankless, job in assisting the Air Corps to accomplish its mission in meeting production schedules and aiding the defense program and war effort by minimizing friction, that at first seemed to spring from thin air.

Mr. Spencer was not only criticized without reason or facts, by some of the white personnel for doing what he was assigned to do, by his superiors, but also was criticized and on several occasions, to my personal knowledge, openly persecuted and embarassed by some Negro personnel and their associates within local communities. The campaign directed against him was so vicious and malicious at one time that he asked the then Commanding General, Harold A. Bartron's permission to challenge the accusations, which were carried on not only verbally by personnel at the Base but through a series of articles in a Negro newspaper, through Civil Court action. But due to the continued war effort General Bartrom felt it would not be deemed advisable. However, at the end of the hostilities of World War II he approved and gave his consent. Mr. Spencer filed suit against the newspaper and nine of the ten witnesses who had given statements to the newspaper, perjured themselves in the trial and the decision was granted in Mr. Spencer's favor. I would like to point out that the results of this case, the employees who made certain allegations regarding Mr. Spencer, were familiar enough to accuse Mr. Spencer of performing irregularities that were violations of Federal regulations, such as, punching out employee's time cards, representing himself as an Officer in the Air Corps, intimidating personnel with threats of personal actions and using his personal influence to effect personnel actions against personnel (Negro) to please his superiors. We found these allegations false and without basis, they were thoroughly investigated and checked.

... Chauncey E. Spencer, in my opinion, has certainly rendered many services to the United States Air Force above and beyond the call of duty, and from the knowledge and information that I and many others, that I know, he has worked under and closely with, are fully aware of the many sacrifices he has made in behalf of the Department of Defense and United States Air Force. From my overall knowledge, through my close working association with Mr. Spencer, as his supervisor, I state, with no reservations that I am firm in my belief that his continued employment with the Department of Defense, United States Air Force, will not constitute a security risk on his part."

The trial was over and I was thankful for that. They had been grueling, long days of mental anguish. Sitting up there on the witness stand having to defend myself against unfounded charges was a humiliating experience. It took all of my patience not to explode at the prosecution's questions, asked over and over in a multitude of slight variations.

Then for six agonizing months, months that we were still subjected to harassment—official silence reigned. Anne and I waited each day hoping to hear of a final settlement. This suspense itself was the ultimate harassment, the fear of the unknown. Finally, on June 29, 1954, I received the following cryptic, clearance letter:

Dear Mr. Spencer:

I am pleased to inform you that the final determination in your case is that, based on all of the available information, your retention in employment is clearly consistent with the interests of national security. This decision has been arrived at and approved in accordance with Air Force Regulation 40-12.

Accordingly, it has been directed that you be restored to your position and that you be paid for the period of your suspension in an amount equal to the difference between the amount you would normally have earned at the rate you were receiving on the date of your suspension and your interim earnings, if any, in accordance with the provisions of Public Law 733, 81st Congress.

BY ORDER OF
THE SECRETARY OF THE AIR FORCE

As formal, as unemotional as the letter was, Anne and I were ecstatic. Finally, the longed for exoneration had come. It was our day of deliverance. Hopefully now, the whispering campaign would end; the harassment would cease. Economically, the clearance came just in time to ward off losing our home and everything we had equity in.

For the storybook and the TV play, here is the perfect ending. The hero is exonerated, old friends cluster round and pound him on the back, and the villains blink out of town in their convertibles. But the forces of intolerance and bigotry are not that easily quelled. Justice, tolerance and fair play must be fought for every day of our lives, as we were soon to discover.

On Tuesday, June 8, 1954, before I received the official letter of clearance on June 29, I received information from Frederick Ayers, Staff Assistant to the Secretary of the Air Force that, "a final determination had been made in your case and you have been cleared of all charges and this information has been sent to the United States Air Force, Headquarters, Director of Personnel in the Pentagon, that you are to be immediately restored to duty . . ." It was never explained why there was a twenty-one day period between the time I was verbally told of my clearance, by Frederick Ayers, and the time I received the letter of notification from Headquarters. It was natural of me to raise questions why there was a delay and I did receive a letter, signed by the Deputy Assistant Secretary of the Air Force James Goode, that I felt sure was directed and written by those in Headquarters, USAF, who had been part of the conspiracy to build up the "security risk" case and have me removed from federal service. This reply only added more questions on my part and my determination to uncover the bigotry and demagoguery involved in my case. However, I did not follow through because an article appeared on the editorial Page of the *Dayton Daily News,* dated Tuesday, July 20, 1954, concerning my case, that disturbed not only Air Force officials but also other top governmental officials. One of my true and proven friends who was a high official called me by telephone and said, ". . . yesterday's article in the *Dayton Daily News* has them all shaking in their boots . . . and it's surely going to really weaken this security risk charging. They are talking of contacting you to find out when you were interviewed by the newspaper. Don't tell them a damn thing. Let them sweat . . . it's too bad you and your family had to suffer this long drawn out affair but it's an ill wind that blows no good. You've come through in flying colors and again you have served your country above and beyond the call of duty. You and Mr. Welsh deserve a lot of credit. . . . (Mr. Joseph Welsh was the celebrated principal trial attorney in the McCarthy hearings who revealed to the American public how the "security risk" charges were being used to bear false witness, defame, slander and "black list" many honest innocent and dedicated Americans.) As soon as I finished talking with my friend, I rushed to get a copy of the editorial regarding my case, which stated:

THE DAYTON DAILY NEWS
TUESDAY, JULY 20, 1954

"TRENDS OF THE TIMES"
PARADOX OF SECURITY:

THE INSECURE CITIZEN

Someone said that Chauncey E. Spencer was a "security risk." Spencer was an employee of the federal government, with a responsible position at Wright Patterson Air Force Base, Ohio.

In these disturbed times with an enemy seeking skillfully to undermine and destroy our way of living and impugn on our people the totalitarian blight, we can take no chances with traitors. We must guard against them with tense care.

When the loyalty of any employee of the government is questioned, no matter by whom, or how, it behooves those responsible to be alert and diligent. What was done in the case of Spencer was alert and diligent enough. With no chance to defend himself he was suspended from his post and his pay was stopped. This sent him forth branded, though the fact was as yet unproved, as a "security risk," a disloyal citizen.

In fairness, he had the privilege, if he could find ways to pay the cost, of appealing his case and proving his innocence. In the interim he was dealt with as if guilty.

One bearing on his brow the brand of disloyalty does not easily find a job in place of the position lost. There has grown up, in these times of panic, a rule of "guilt by association." Who employs or consorts with one charged with disloyalty incurs himself the charge of disloyalty.

The accused in this case could find no employment while he appealed his case. How could he pay the cost of such appeal? His right to appeal was permission to go a-swimming:

'Hang your clothes on a hickory limb, and don't go near the water.'

This man did manage to carry up his case. At the end of 10 months a decision was dispatched. He had proved his innocence. He could have his old job back, together with the last 10 months' pay. Justice was finally done.

Justice?

He was declared innocent. His lost wages were repaid.

PUNISHED THOUGH INNOCENT

Yet, though innocent, he had been terribly punished as if guilty. He had been made to suffer months of mental torture. He had been caused to live as a leper among his neighbors. Can one robbed of his good name ever gain the jewel he has lost?

On what evidence was this innocent man singled out for this misfortune, this punishment? It could have been only the imagining of the ignorant or the malevolent.

The men who wrote our Constitution were aware of such danger to the innocent citizen. They had had their experience with tyrants and sought with care to guard the right of men to justice and security. A totalitarian tyranny will call men guilty till they prove themselves innocent. Our country should have none of that.

Yet here a mere whisper from some disordered minds can have been the source of Chauncey Spencer's 10 months of torment and disgrace. To be suspected, as our efforts at security go, is to be treated as if guilt were proved.

To reduce the menace to citizens of accusations idly or malevolently made, they saw to it a grand jury must consider in secret all charges made to assure their probable truth before the bar. No irresponsible whisper, no addled witch hunter, should have power to disgrace and impoverish an innocent citizen.

The mind of the citizen, like his house, was to be his castle. The accused could not be made to testify against himself. A mighty safeguard much assailed in these excited times. The accused had the right to confront his accusers.

So determined the Fathers were to protect the citizen from injury by personal enemies or by the state.

Now the question of 'security' of the state against infiltrating enemies comes counter to that of security of its citizens. Now we cope with men's minds, their tendencies, not with their acts.

Because a "poor security risk" must be removed before he has time to act we find ourselves, in the name of security for the nation, assailing the security of the citizen.

GUILT BY ACCUSATION

No presentment of grand jury, to careful weighing of evidence, precedes the punishment meted out to the alleged "security risk." Merely to express a suspicion of a citizen is here to precipitate his loss of employment and reputation, however blameless he be, this is not America. We think of the totalitarianRussian, cowering behind his door, awaiting the knock that tells the secret police have come. In Russia only? Not in America where men, especially in Congress, claim headlines and glory and votes by shouting to all the world irresponsible accusations such as brought this woe to Chauncey Spencer. How safe is any American Citizen, especially if he be in the Army or working for the government?

Such is the problem of the people's security which the search for national security precipitates. We have held that a man is innocent till he is proved guilty. Now we see men punished as if guilty till they prove themselves innocent. We have said, "Better 10 guilty escape than one innocent should suffer." Now 10 innocent are made to suffer lest one guilty escape.

Surely, there must be a way to protect the nation's security without thus destroying the citizen's security. To defeat the Communists, need we act like the Communists?"—WALTER LOCKE

* * *

A PLAGUE OF INFORMERS
The Washington Post and Times-Herald

It is a heartening reality to have the Department of Justice investigating the possibility of perjury on the part of the informers who recently made irresponsible charges against Ralph Bunche, leading American Member of the United Nations Secretariat. Dr. Bunche was unanimously cleared. His accusers, professed former Communists, are employees of that informers' haven, the Justice Department's Immigration and Naturalization Service.

Dr. Bunche escaped the calumny of these men because, by good fortune, he found an old acquaintance who had the fortitude and decency to come forward, acknowledge the errors of his own political past and refute the charge made by the informers. It is in the area of political heterodoxy that the role of the professional informer is bound to be a malevolent one. Persons who give information to the police about conventional crimes, of course, render a service to society, and law enforcement authorities can usefully avail themselves of such information since it becomes subject to the exacting checks of due process in courts of law. But the allegations of political informers are not usually subject to such checks. In loyalty and security hearings, they are rarely required to face the rigors of cross-examinations: often, indeed, neither the accused nor his judges knows the identity of the accusers. Thus, there is no way to measure the reliability of the informer, no way to determine whether he is malicious or prejudiced or even perhaps, despite his protestations of apostasy, still an undercover member of the Communist conspiracy striving to sow confusion and deprive the country of the services of able public officials. These obvious drawbacks place a special obligation upon government if it makes use of informers to check on whether they are telling the truth and to prosecute them where they are not.

I do know there were several conferences regarding the editorial but if any Air Force or other officials contacted the *Dayton Daily News* it was never mentioned.

CHAPTER SIX

THE HAPPINESS OVER MY CLEARANCE AND RE-
turn to my former position was short lived. My superiors
who had helped clear me were a minority against others
whose emotions against me had been stirred by the flames
of panic, ignorance and bigotry—for these are the inevitable
results whenever the Government brings security charges,
regardless of the final outcome. For some, the accusations
themselves were sufficient proof of my guilt.

Furthermore, those superiors who had stood by me and
had been the cause of my clearance, were soon accosted by
remarks and unfavorable actions from high Air Force
sources. A part of the price of my exoneration was the
knowledge that I had blighted the careers of some of my best
friends. Charles E. Crutchfield, then OSI agent, now Professor of Law at Notre Dame University, in South Bend,
Indiana, had his career put in jeopardy because he aided my
defense. In the midst of my case he was suddenly shipped
out to Japan, disrupting his study of law in the evening.
Such situations do not make for happy working conditions.

And at home for my wife and at school for my son, exoneration did not prove a release from bondage. The ignorant
cruelty that parents practice is well-reflected in their off
spring. My son was still bullied; my wife still received
ominous phone calls; our lawn was still a target for garbage
and debris.

95

In an effort to escape this torturous psychological aura that was smothering us, I applied for the position of Placement Officer, GS-9, at Cherbourg, France, an Air Materiel Area base. Although at this time I was a GS-11 with two years experience as a Placement and Employee Relations Officer, I was willing to accept a lower-ranking position just to escape the oppressive atmosphere surrounding us. Because of my qualifications and my experience with AMC, I was selected for the position. My papers were processed and I was alerted to prepare for shots and passport application. Then, the blow fell—the mask was ripped away from those officials at the Personnel Office of Headquarters USAF whose claim was that the charges against me had been brought in the interest of protecting the Government. Wright-Patterson Air Force Base had sent to Headquarters USAF for a shipment number to send me and my family to Cherbourg to fill the Placement Officer vacancy which existed there. A TWX, a telegram between installations, came back, unsigned, from Headquarters USAF to Headquarters AMC directing overseas officials to select another person to fill the vacancy because I was not qualified! This was an unprecedented action to Wright-Patterson Field which, hitherto, had final selection approval for all overseas vacancies in Air Materiel Command. Never before had Headquarters USAF, on the basis of qualifications, even questioned a selection of its overseas officials for an overseas vacancy! John A. Watts and his staff, especially Harry O. Carr, were, obviously, pressing again to keep me "in my place." Their personal vendetta knew no bounds.

After this illustration of the venom directed at me by higher headquarters, working conditions became more painful and embarassing day by day.

I was not the only one, however, who suffered. The Honorable Harold Talbott, then Secretary of the Air Force, was angered over the collusion and conspiracy against me and made a statement to me in my visit to his Washington office in the Pentagon building that the action was "unwarranted, and uncalled for . . ." He also said it was his intention to take action and "let the chips fall where they may" concerning those guilty of any part in my case. He expected some "heads to roll in the Air Force," and he further said, "I am going to start in the Directorate of Personnel, Headquarters, USAF."

As a result of his verbal commitment, he was approached by three Congressional members, who tried to compromise him. They urged him not to make a scandal and embarass certain Air Force officials because of the Spencer case—or they would expose his conflicts of interests. (Secretary Talbott had several business interests and investments in industrial operations, and contracts had come through USAF office employing those companies.)

Talbott challenged the Congressmen, ignoring their threat: "Look and Listen Well. As long as I'm Secretary of the Air Force, *I* run the Air Force, and I suggest to you gentlemen, that you go back on the hill and try to run your Congress."

With that he proceeded to make known his intentions to initiate reprimands and make changes in personnel. The Congressmen also made good their threats of exposure and it was detrimental to the Secretary of the Air Force Talbott.

Conflict of interest charges were brought against Secretary Talbott by the Senate.

* * *

On August 11, 1955, I sent him a telegram expressing my appreciation for his action in my behalf; it took more than military courage to do what he did knowing what the consequences could be.

I received, in return, a letter from him that read:

Dear Mr. Spencer:

Thank you very much for your very kind telegram of August 11th. My wife and I left Washington on the 13th for Southampton, Long Island for a much needed rest, and I returned to my New York office only yesterday; therefore my tardy reply to your nice message.

I truly believe that during my tenure as Secretary, the Air Force has gained in public stature and maturity. I know it has become a tougher fighting organization.

To my utmost regret, the distorted and unfair publicity placed me in the unacceptable position of causing
embarassment to our great President and his Administration. In those circumstances, I felt it necessary to resign.
Again, let me thank you for the nice things you say
in your letter and for your thoughtfulness in wiring me.
                                        Sincerely yours,
                                        H. E. Talbott

Later, it became known that President Eisenhower had
requested his resignation. It was approximately six months
later that Harold E. Talbott, laboring under these pressures,
suffered a fatal heart attack in New York.

His name will always be remembered by me as one who
truly represented what his country is supposed to stand for;
the equality of man and the right to be respected—and he
had the courage to stand up and be counted.

In desperation, hearing of an opening at the GS-7 level
in the personnel field at Norton Air Force Base in California,
I applied for it, though it meant a salary cut of approximately $3,000 per year.

CHAPTER SEVEN

THOSE USAF OFFICIALS WHO HAD TRIED TO RE-move me from my job were glad to see me accept the job offer in California. I had not accepted graciously my security clearance. Why should I? Actually, nothing had changed. I wrote to several Congressmen (including Charles Diggs and Adam Clayton Powell), to *Time* magazine, to high govern-ment officials explaining what had happened. There were a number of "first letter high promises" from Washington—even telephone calls of interest and concern. Still, nothing came of it.

And so, despite the tremendous salary loss, it was with a great sense of relief that my wife Anne, my then five chil-dren and I packed our belongings and moved, at government expense of eight thousand dollars, to San Bernardino, California.

Not long afterwards, on a rainy March afternoon, Anne and I saw the house we decided to call home. Albeit weather-beaten, it reminded me very much of my Lynchburg home that my father had built for his family seventy-two years past. The rain poured down on this huge, two story wood-frame house whose shutters were flapping in the wind giving the eerie effect of a haunted house. The broken windows, drooping eaves, the holes in the floor of the porch couldn't deter Anne. Her mind was made up—the house had charm and beauty underneath the dilapidated exterior.

With financial help from my father, we bought the seventy-year-old home for $6,500. Little did we know at the time, that a condemnation order would soon appear in our window, not because the structure was not in basically good condition, but because a San Bernardino city building inspector did not want my family in the white neighborhood. City housing inspectors ordered a complete rebuilding of the house if we did not want it destroyed. We completely hulled out the inside—re-plastering, re-wiring, re-doing the plumbing. We even had to remove many of the 2 x 4 beams and replace them with 2 x 6 beams. All total, we did eighteen thousand dollars worth of remodeling, but we were happy. It was now the home we had always wanted, painted crisp white with a huge swing on the winding porch that stretched across two sides of the house.

Later, the house was featured in the San Bernardino *Sun-Telegram*. That article, titled, "A House That Tells Stories Of The Past," told how the house had once served as an Old Men's Home for the Salvation·Army, later being turned into an apartment building, and later still, into a dance hall featuring live orchestras.

Our home was, and still is furnished in antiques collected throughout our entire married life. As a result of antique auction sales, we've garnered our collection piecemeal beginning with copper pieces given to us by my mother. We have a veritable museum; a cross-section ranging from brass beds to a piano from a torn down English Pub to an Italian grandfather clock. Our furnishings are now a far cry from those during our early married years when Anne draped crates in order to have the appearance of tables and chairs. "Oh, no, don't sit on that," she would say if anyone looked like they were about to sit on the decorative but flimsy, chairs. Those were days of floor-sitting.

From 1956 to 1959, I worked at Norton Air Force Base, as an Employee Relations Officer, only this time at the GS-7 level. The pressure was still a burden, though, with a court case, initiated by me against those who had perjured themselves in my security risk trial, still to be decided and with bills from our nearly bankrupt Dayton days still hounding us.

In 1959, at age fifty-three, I decided to leave the Air Force. Mounting pressures were taking their toll with my health. I qualified for a retirement pension, having served the government for thirty-two years, including twenty-two years of service with the U.S. Air Force. I submitted my resignation. For the next three years, I was a part-time janitor but, never to be deterred from problem-solving situations, I was also actively involved in the community of San Bernardino as its Human Relations Officer.

In 1962 I became the security officer at San Bernardino High School. Unlike many other jobs with the same title, this job was more comprehensive. Besides the customary duties as security officer, the job involved covering classes for absent teachers, being involved in school policy meetings and serving as part of the faculty.

It was an intriguing job for me to work in this school of 2,400 students of whom thirty percent were Negro. A tremendous opportunity was to be had by observing from inside the schools the changes taking place in the high schools of the 1960's.

Pressure was further enhanced, though, when my father died in 1964. As the *Lynchburg News* reported at his death, "The death of Edward A. Spencer at the age of eighty-eight years removes one of Lynchburg's most respected, exemplary citizens, to all who knew him well enough to be aware of his quality."

I have always been well-aware of my father's gentleness, his innate respect for other human beings. His character was one to be patterned after and one that I can look to with pride and respect.

After serving as security officer at San Bernardino High School for six years, I was transferred to San Gorgonio High School because the newly-assigned principal, George Dibs, and I did not agree on his views of handling ethnic and/or minority students.

Not long after I had begun the job at San Gorgonio High School, there occurred a two hour campus riot at this school. What had begun as a small fight with sixteen or seventeen students hitting each other and pelting rocks, ended with well over a hundred students involved. By the time the police arrived, many of the students were hurt and had to be hospitalized.

Suddenly, in the midst of the commotion, everyone became an expert on "Negro problems." Some whites, whose only direct contact with Negroes was what they heard from their maids, used their maid's few utterings about Negroes as if they were psychologists. Problem solvers and "experts" seemed to pop up everywhere. So-called Negroes and whites from the kitchens to the colleges began dropping names such as Frederick Douglass, George Washington Carver, Ralph Bunche and Sojourner Truth. Everyone had an instant solution and knew the best way of handling the rock-throwing melee.

Including myself, I, along with two vice-principals and other members of the faculty, urged the principal and top administrators to take a hard-line approach. We needed some get-tough tactics. Instead, the administrators, all of whom were white, agreed on an appeasement policy. Whereas I would have suspended the troublemakers, those sixteen or seventeen Negro and white students well-known to all of us, the administrators appeased them. They invited the Negro instigators to "rap" at a series of dinners. White administrators, fearful of some belligerent Negro students, would look the other way if they saw a Negro sauntering down the hall ordering students out of his way and into the doorways. Small gangs of Negro students would go on "hunts" to fight other students of both races, and the maligned students at the other high schools would retaliate with fights with the Negro students. The situation was out of hand, but still the students were appeased. And ultimately, the Negro students relished the power they could exert and the submission they could command.

Overbearing and threatening Negro parents and students were appeased in other of their demands, too. They were given Black studies, a reversal to segregation. I complained to administrators: "I'm not going back to segregation—to

Black studies, to Black dormitories, to Black schools. I've worked all my life for integration and now we're retreading our steps. There's no such thing as 'Black history!' Those Negroes who contributed of their talent, did so as Americans, not because their skin color was a shade darker than a white man's. The Negroes' contribution to history should be taught, and *must* be taught, but not as a separate entity. Negro history is part of American history and should be taught that way. 'Black history' is just another way of saying keep a Negro in his place, tantamount to 'Jim Crow;' 'Appalachia,' too, is similar; it says keep a poor white in his place. I maintain that there's going to be racial strife in this country as long as there is a license to call anyone 'Black' or 'Negro.' I am a full-blooded American—a composite, the same as many other Americans, 'white' or otherwise. To be called 'Black' might give some so-called Negroes a personal sense of security but it tags him; it sets him apart. 'Separate but equal' was ruled unconstitutional long ago."

My admonitions fell on deaf ears. Separate Black study courses were introduced at not only San Bernardino High School and San Gorgonio High School but at many high schools through the nation in the 1960's. America seems to be working at cross-purposes—with busing attempting to bring the races together and Black studies to set them apart. In frustration, I wired Roy Wilkins, Executive Director of the NAACP, National Office New York City. I had been president of the local San Bernardino NAACP chapter. My telegram read:

I will and am available to serve as plaintiff to block the creation of autonomous Black studies programs and Black student dormitories on college campuses. I have fully supported the NAACP program to get Negro history courses taught in elementary, high school and college courses. My opposition to the autonomous "Black" studies program has been of long standing and resulted in my being dubbed as "controversial" in this local area. I see many dangers and setbacks in the students' actions of "special" Black demands. There is major support in

103

this area and state in the NAACP program. I have also long advocated against the use of "race" by the Federal Government, FBI, etc. in reference to minority groups and minorities. It is not needed. Americans must apply to all and within a short span of time all hyphenated racial descriptions will disappear.

Roy Wilkins' reply was an encouraging one to me. It reinforced my views and reminded me, once again, that I was not in this fight alone, despite my lifelong arguments with both Negroes and whites on racial matters. When I took the time to really think about it, I knew that the huge majority of the twenty-two million Negroes in this country were supporters of the NAACP's and my views. I was not in isolation, nor was I a lone dissenter whose voice cried out to a vacuum.

Negroes wanted the same things in their lives as whites did. Despite the militant rhetoric, aspirations of both races transcended the color of skin. Negroes wanted opportunities to work; they wanted good schools for their children; they wanted a society that was not crime-ridden; they wanted to own homes and property. The "more moderate" Negroes had to remind themselves of these facts when, particularly during the late 1960's, the militant Negroes were highly vocal and claiming to be "The Spokesmen" for the entire Negro people. These militants have not realized that these are problems that didn't just happen today. There are thousands of Americans, long before me and like me, who have been combatting racial prejudice every day of their lives. And progress *has* been made. It was a slow process, to be sure, but we did not, and will not, overcome racism by overthrowing the government, or by disobeying laws, or by becoming more segregated. It was during these outspoken, militant times, that we so-called moderates took succor from Roy Wilkins' responses:

Dear Mr. Spencer:

Thank you for your telegram supporting our opposition to the setting up of Jim Crow dormitories and autonomous Jim Crow black studies centers in campuses throughout the country.

Despite the plain language employed, efforts are already underway to misrepresent our stand as one "blocking black students" or as one "opposing the teaching of Negro history."

We support the teaching of Negro history, the employment of more Negro teachers and the enrollment of more Negro College students. We do not support Jim Crow, whether it is proposed by whites or blacks.

We repeat the NAACP believes court action is indicated when any tax-supported college or university, or any institution public, or private, which receives grants from tax funds, agrees to set up what will be in reality separate Jim Crow black campuses within established campuses and further agrees to grant black students autonomy in the running of studies centers.

Autonomy means the hiring and firing of teachers and other officials, the approval of curricula and control of the budget, the institution itself having nothing to say about the so-called Black Studies Centers.

This would be a Jim Crow school set up with public funds. We do not believe that under present laws and customs, tax money can be used for racist segregation.

Very sincerely yours
Roy Wilkins
Executive Director

It is little understood that the NAACP has never condoned civil rights tactics which smack of a return to racial separation. They have opposed separate Black history, the study of Black English, and "Buy Black" consumerism. They have countered these trends with an insistence on the rightful place of the Black man in the mainstream of American culture.

In the community-at-large I found racial retrenchment. There were many instances in the community that reflected its prejudice. Often, I would bring these occurrences to the attention of the Chief of Police, the City Council and the

San Bernardino Human Relations Commission. I was getting to be known in the community, by those who disagreed with me, as a troublemaker, a rabble rouser, and a "behind the scenes" riot inciter.

One particular example of false reporting racism and bigotry inflamed me. On September 23, 1963, the local paper, the *Sun-Telegram,* San Bernardino, California, carried the headlined column, "200 Youths Hurl Stones at Officers in San Bernardino Riot." A "full-scale riot erupted" . . . the paper reported. "At the height of the riot, the youths virtually 'took over' the block, breaking into homes, tearing up shrubbery, hurling bottles and rocks through windows. . . ."

The truth is that the "riot" simply did not happen. A thorough fact-finding investigation of the alleged occurrence proved to be non-existent. Residents in the so-called riot knew nothing about it. I brought this to the attention of Mayor Donald Maudlin, mayor of the city. He disregarded the evidence and, instead, told news reporters, "Don't have anything to say about this. He doesn't know what he's talking about."

Discouraged at the lack of support in the mayor's office, I went directly to the man ultimately responsible for the reporting, the editor of the *Sun-Telegram.* Presented with substantial evidence, he admitted partial guilt but said, "We can't afford to retract it. One of our reporters just became overzealous. I'd advise you not to say anything more about it or you'll be shot out of the saddle."

Later, as Police Commissioner, I learned that this reported riot was purposely contrived in order to induce a negative psychological effect in the Negro community. Three John Birch members of the Police Department had leaked news of the riot to the newspaper in hopes of inciting foment among the Negroes. The John Birch Society, with its stronghold for the "Impeach Earl Warren" campaign in California, was strong in San Bernardino as well as in Orange County.

I went to one John Birch meeting in San Bernardino where they showed a 35 mm. film of clips of movies taken completely out of context. They superimposed pictures of

Martin Luther King linked arm in arm with known Communists leading Civil Rights marches.

A chance to make the city more responsive to its problems came in 1965. A mayoral election between incumbent Donald "Bud" Maudlin and Al Ballard, also white, gave me hope for a change. Al Ballard, knowing of my frequent appearances before the San Bernardino City Council, approached me by saying he was very interested in my one-man fight and would appreciate my support in the forthcoming election.

I knew little about Al at this time, but as I was vociferously opposed to the racist Maudlin, I decided to give my support to Al. I campaigned for him, giving speeches and appearing with him. With his pledge to change the racial situation in San Bernardino, I grew to respect this former fireman who was straightforward and honest.

Al Ballard won the election and became San Bernardino's mayor. One of his first acts was to select me as Police Commissioner, an appointment which needed the approval of the City Council. After a great deal of debate, I barely received the appointment by a three to two margin.

There immediately arose a furor in the police department. The police were fearful of drastic changes within the department now that I was Police Commissioner. As a result of my being actively involved in the city, the police were well aware of my ideas. No drastic changes were made, however. The John Birchers within the department that I had compiled facts and data on resigned and left of their own accord. The department continued as an effective service to the community.

One of the major issues that developed while I was Police Commissioner involved arming the city firemen with shotguns. Al Ballard wanted to arm them in order to insure their protection, an increasing problem as both youths and adults sometimes hurled rocks as firemen tried to battle a blaze. Once in a while, a shot even rang out. Firemen, symbols of the racist establishment, were easy targets for aroused youths in neighborhoods affected by arson and rioting. I felt that the police could give ample protection to the firemen. Arming firemen would simply create more tension in an already racially tense city. The argument attracted NBC news and I was spotlighted on the Huntley-Brinkley newscast. Eventually, the argument turned in favor of my position and the firemen were not armed.

Problems with libelous newspapers sprang up again in 1965 when the local Negro newspaper, the *Precinct Reporter*, ran an article directed at me, though not naming me personally. Samuel Martin (who I later discovered had had the job of keeping a former police chief informed on "Negro attitudes and actions" in the community) wrote the column, "The Inland Eye" which read:

> It's time the Westside citizens put an end to outsiders running their affairs. As you know, one carpetbagger that lives just east of the freeway, near downtown, is constantly meddling. The big question is why? When the records show that he doesn't live in the 6th Ward, but has been chosen by the people downtown to represent the Negro.
>
> It may be also interesting to know that this controversial carpetbagger has questionable background starting at Wright-Patterson Air Force Base in the state of Ohio.
>
> According to some sources, this individual was investigated to find out whether he had alliances with the Communist party. So my friends beware of the head hunter; he is a professional in character assassinations; he will cry peace out of the left side of his mouth, with a dagger in his right hand.

TEST FOR OUTSTANDING CITIZENS:

1. Have you ever sued the NAACP for $400 or less?

(I had lent the local NAACP $400 to pay some bills and later they refused to pay me back. I brought the case to court but the $400 was paid back to me in an out-of-court settlement.)

2. Do you have a son or daughter in prison?

(My seventeen-year-old son was in California Youth Authority custody for incorrigibility and petty thefts.)

3. Have you ever been investigated by the Air Force or the U.S. Government because you appeared to have Communist ties?
4. Do you drive an official car that's paid for by the taxpayers to take care of your personal and private business?
4b. How many official cars have you wrecked within the last 18 months?
5. Do you write a column for a newspaper, weekly or daily?

(I was writing a weekly column for the San Bernardino *Tribune,* a paper put out for the mayor, Al Ballard, to counter some of the allegations in the opposing San Bernardino paper, the *Sun-Telegram* and the *Precinct Reporter.* I wrote the column while Police Commissioner and titled it "The Watchman."

If all of your answers are yes, 'watch out' the people are watching you.

If your answers are no, don't worry, you don't need a 'watchman.'

The sensational, tabloid-type taunts of the newspaper could not go unchallenged. They cleverly implied a moral unfitness which they would not dare to charge directly. Another of the *Precinct Reporter's* issues featured caricatures titled Chauncey Spencer saying, "I'se gwanna be top dog in the Urban League and don ye forgot it." The article accompanying read "The people are saying 'A person who has lost the confidence of the people so completely as Chauncey Spencer is hardly a true representative of the people.' "

I filed suit in superior court San Bernardino County claiming conspiracy to defame me on the part of the publisher Art Townsend and reporter Sam Martin. The defendants claimed that the articles were not libelous because they were based on truth and did not mention me specifically.

Although I was awarded $3,500 for the second time in my life by a libelous newspaper, the defendants were not satisfied with the verdict. They attempted to overturn the jury's verdict by appealing to a higher court. The local San Bernardino NAACP branch, which during this time was taken over by militants who had previously been anti-NAACP, sided with the defendants and felt so strongly about the justice of the verdict that they voted to spearhead a drive to raise funds for the appeal.

I immediately objected. I brought the proposed use of the funds to the attention of the national office. The national NAACP wrote to the local branch attempting to raise the funds, "There is no way in which this could become the legitimate official action of the local NAACP branch. It is not a civil rights matter; it has to do solely with a private quarrel in which one party claims to have been slandered by another party and in which the court has agreed with the accuser. . . . The inappropriateness of the branch action is . . . evident."

It was unfortunate, and yet perhaps ultimately beneficial, that the court case burgeoned into a divisiveness between the local NAACP branch and the national organization. The branch, through which Sam Martin and Arthur Townsend were working, was now wholly controlled by militants. The rest of us were expected to agree with the philosophy and join their activities or face their ridicule, harassment and abuse in the form of being called a traitor or an Uncle Tom, an epithet I would rather prefer to be called than a "Tom Fool."

Ultimately, the national NAACP ruling took precedence and the local chapter did not raise the money for an appeal of the newspaper case that I had originally won.

Concurrent with my job as Police Commissioner, I obtained an Avis Franchise in 1968. This was an enterprise the entire family, some of whom were now high school age, could participate in. We rented a car lot about a mile from our home and set up an office emblazoned in the red and white Avis colors. Sometimes we'd have as many as twenty-five to thirty cars there. It was a thriving business largely because

Norton Air Force Base was near and many personnel would fly to the base and then rent a car to drive to Los Angeles, fifty-two miles to the west of San Bernardino.

Our main problem in running the business was that it was a twenty-four hour operation. Invariably, the phone rang at two or three A.M. and then two of us, one to drive the Avis car to the prospective renter and one to drive the two of us back to the house, would have to get up and leave in the middle of the night.

This same year that we held the Avis franchise, I traveled by plane to Lynchburg, Virginia to visit my mother. Thinking that it would be convenient to rent a car while staying in Lynchburg, I called ahead to the Avis dealer in that city and was promised a car would be waiting for me. But when I arrived at the Avis counter in the airport, I was refused service. I told the dealer that I had been promised a car. I explained that I was the Police Commissioner of San Bernardino. Neither explanation did any good. I presented my credentials. "I don't care who the hell you are. I'm not going to rent you a car." I wasn't going to give him my trump card—that I was also an Avis agent the same as he.

Hearing the increasingly vocal argument we were engaged in, the Hertz dealer, one counter removed, called to me, "Look mister, I see what you're facing. We'll rent you a car." And so I drove the Hertz car, but not without vociferous complaint to the holder of the Avis franchise in Richmond, Virginia. The New York Avis public relations office claimed that they were sorry but that they had no control over actions of individual dealers; however, if I would go to Roanoke, Virginia, they would see that a car was available "at no extra charge to you." Avis remained "number two" and they did not "try harder."

In 1970, fortune fell my way and I was offered the position of Deputy Administrator for the Michigan city of Highland Park, a suburb of Detroit. For me, psychologically, there really was no choice in the matter of whether or not to accept the job. Although we were doing financially well with the Avis franchise, it was not something I really could be enthused about, particularly after my hometown Avis

111

incident. Money was not my main concern. I wanted a job where I could continue to create an impact; effect a change; influence some people to the idea that the color of one's skin or where he was born did not keep him from being a good American—nor did it make him one.

Anne had some misgivings about the proposed move—our six-month-old Avis franchise was just beginning to be lucrative; I had been re-appointed to another four year term as Police Commissioner; our growing family of eight children were settled and satisfied in the warm California weather.

We had been told little about Highland Park; we even had to get out our Atlas to see where it was located—but the lure of the $23,000-a-year job and its attendant responsibility was one, in the final analysis, I couldn't turn down at my age, now sixty-five.

CHAPTER EIGHT

LIKE EVERYWHERE ELSE I'VE EVER BEEN, HIGH-
land Park has its racial problems. Situated like an island
with the City of Detroit surrounding it, Highland Park has
become predominantly Negro as whites moved out to the
suburbs, and now even further in their exodus as Negroes,
limited by de facto housing segregation to a minimal number of areas, tried to escape the Detroit ghettos.

Highland Park was once a wooded haven on the northern
fringe of Detroit's urban growth. It still straddles Woodward
Avenue, a major artery to the prosperous suburbs of Oak-
land County, but the street which boasted the first mile of
concrete pavement and which passes the historic Highland
Park plant at which the early "T" and "A" models of Fords
were mass-produced has itself been bypassed by the motor
city's shoppers and commuters. Adult movie houses and
vacant store fronts dot the avenue as witness to its deteri-
orated state. Commuters clog the Lodge and Chrysler Free-
ways between Detroit and the white outer suburbs. These
sterile concrete routes completely bypass Highland Park.

I arrived to work in Highland Park on the thirteenth of
July, 1970. At four-thirty that afternoon, Dan Chiz, the
Director of Personnel, called me and asked me to meet him
immediately at the Highland Park Police Department.
Mayor Robert B. Blackwell happened to be out of town on

113

a business trip and trouble was quickly developing in the city. I met Dan Chiz and found that a full-scale riot had developed at a bar on the corner of Hamilton and Avalon in Highland Park. An argument between the white owner and a Negro customer had resulted in the owner shooting and killing the customer in front of the bar. People had gathered around, fights were breaking out and windows of area stores were being pelted. Passing cars and area homes quickly became rock targets. The mob was growing and looting had begun. This was going to be a difficult job for the nearly all-white Highland Park Police force. By seven o'clock state and local law enforcement officers had cordoned off the area and an eleven o'clock curfew was established.

Past experience had proven that a curfew with quick arrests of violators was the best means of quelling a disturbance. The civil rebellion of July, 1967, had caught Detroit, Michigan and the United States of America in a state of almost complete unpreparedness. The conflagration had spread beyond easy control while precious hours were squandered in a frantic effort to decide what should be done and who should do it. Highland Park was also inevitably entangled in the 1968 disturbance which followed the killing of Dr. Martin Luther King. These two civic crises left police and civil officials united and ready to react. This was no time to linger, rush hour traffic coming back from Detroit via Hamilton Avenue was heavy.

The bar and building were destroyed by fire, but by midnight the streets were cleared of people, thru traffic moved normally, and at daybreak the next morning Highland Park was peaceful and quiet. . . . It was Sunday, July 14, 1970.

That proved to be a quick introduction into the problems besetting Highland Park. There had been no time to acquaint myself with the city, to discover the specific ills beleaguering it. Somehow, though, the patterns seemed all-too-familiar.

I didn't feel that President Nixon was helping the problem among Americans when he pointed out color and racial patterns as he did on January 4, 1971 when he said on network television in reference to Dr. Patrick Moynihan, ". . .

He was not referring to neglect for Black Americans or any Americans." Any reference to race or color that indicates a difference between Americans is dangerous; it aggravates and perpetuates racial stereotypes.

After hearing and watching President Nixon on television on January 4, 1971, I felt that as an American I should write him and let him know my thoughts. On January 7, 1971 I wrote the following letter to the President:

My Dear Mr. President:

My family and I watched and listened with great interest and concern to an hour's conversation between you and your network correspondents on television Monday night, January 4, 1971.

We are American Citizens, and on being citizens by birth with deep rooted strong loyalties, allegiance and heritage, we were not only disturbed but alarmed at your reference in behalf of Dr. Patrick Moynihan in which you stated, ". . . He was not referring to neglect for Black Americans or any Americans." Sir, in our opinion, as well as many other Americans, any reference of race-color that indicates or points a difference in or between Americans is dangerous and violates the principles of our democracy. This is especially true when expressed and endorsed by our President. We ask you by what standards within our democracy are Americans classified and determined by color? Americans must not continue to be led blindly from one generation to another into a false sense of security and inferiority, through variable brain washings of color, race, creed or national origin.

During the World War II period a national magazine reported in an article, as a result of a survey, "200,000 Negroes a year cross the color line." The article further stated that over a period of a year two hundred thousand American Negroes from southern states with very light skin, some with blond hair and blue eyes, others with very fair complexions, who were subjected to the economic pressures, insults and prejudices of other southern Americans, migrated to the North and lost their racial identity into the so-called white race. Mr. President, that was thirty and forty years in the past. Our parents have told us this type of migration happened many decades prior to the aforementioned published article. Therefore, twenty years multiplied by two hundred thousand would produce four million, which could be multiplied by two additional generations. This certainly allows thought to the fact that reports on our late President Warren Gamaliel Harding, Marion, Ohio, 1865-1923, our twenty-ninth President, may have been a product of "the American migration"—and Mr. President, as of this date, who else —an unknown unaccountable number. We believe it is now the time we are classified as Americans—and not by race, color, creed or national origin.

This brings to my mind a statement made by you in the outer city surrounding our home, Detroit, Michigan, on the 15th of February, 1960, ". . . America cannot afford the sheer economic waste of racial intolerance." The reference to an American by color, regardless of those who think it "fashionable" or "the in-thing" in "identity." It only continues to aggravate, aggrieve and perpetuate differences between and among Americans.

Since this network television conversation we have talked with our "fellow-Americans" of many sections and variations of life, they all agree that they do not want to be classified by color or race different than that of an American. However, we would be remiss if we did not consider those individuals who over the past four or five years who feel it necessary and "in order" to describe Americans by the "fashionable" or "in-thing" according to color.

Mr. President over the past five generations of American history there are a very few of us who are certain of our ancestors. Once when a reporter asked Mrs. Eleanor Roosevelt if it was true, as it had been reported that she was sympathetic to the Negro cause and plight in America because she had Negro blood in her lineage, Mrs. Roosevelt replied, "I don't know. I can only trace my ancestors back to the 17th century . . ."

Mr. President, Sir, this letter is sent to you in an objective and informative manner of respect and purpose. It is hoped that it can, through you and your office, contribute better hope, good-will and understanding to our fellow-Americans.

Respectfully yours,
Chauncey E. Spencer

I did receive a reply which was short, permissive and prescribed from an Administrative Assistant to the President, R. E. Cushman. "The President acknowledges your letter dated January 7, 1971. He thanks you for writing to him." Six months later I was called in by the Internal Revenue Office for an audit . . . and also in 1972, 1973 and 1974.

We as American citizens hold the American flag close and dear to our hearts, but feel it is a phony gesture to wrap ourselves in it and shout law and order to hoodwink other Americans.

And who can be sure of racial denotations or genes? Thousands upon thousands of southern Americans migrated North and lost their racial identity in the white race. Who dares to bare the shameful pages of history of these United States and its citizens looking back over the past five generations? The distinctions become irrelevant, and moreover, unnecessary. Let us all be called Americans and let us be taught American history, which includes people, all human beings.

In 1973, sixty-eight percent of the city of Highland Park was Negro, albeit ninety-eight percent of the school children were Negro in the Highland Park schools. It was indicative of the trend in the schools. Many parents, white and Negro, who weren't leaving the city were fearful for their school-age children and concerned about the schools' very low achievement level, as indicated in yearly, state-wide testing. Both whites and some Negroes were finding alternative methods of education—either costly private schools or different school districts for which they would also have to pay extra fees.

Unfortunately an incident which occurred shortly after

117

I moved my family to Highland Park is an example of the way whites and Negroes interact in the school system. My daughter, LuJuan, was sitting on a bench at school one day when three Negro boys approached her. Without any explanation, one of them stepped forward and hit her in the face so hard she was knocked off the bench. We finally discovered that part of the initiation rites for an all Negro club was for the prospective member to hit a white girl. LuJuan's appearance reflects the fact that she has a fraternal grandmother who is an Indian and a maternal grandfather who is white.

A real moral dilemma arises in our home each time Anne and I discuss whether or not our five children who are still at home (some are now married or away in college) should continue to attend the Highland Park schools. Anne, who is more protective of our children, is of the opinion that we should find an alternative. The school system is a poor one and there are many racial problems, particularly with our fifteen-year-old son who is sometimes called "half-breed" or "oreo," a reference to the Oreo cookie with the chocolate exterior and the white interior. Anne says, "Sure, in theory, it sounds good not to abandon the schools so they can decline even more. But our children are the ones who are suffering. We're expecting them to come out of high school and make something of themselves when they don't have the academic background. I'm sure some of LuJuan's trouble at Kalamazoo College is because she didn't receive the proper subjects and training her last two years before she graduated from Highland Park High School. She was an "A" student in California. She's really a smart girl but how can she compete with other students who have gotten very good academic training?"

LuJuan went to Kalamazoo College, a highly respected smaller school in Michigan. After a year there she returned to the large Wayne State University in Detroit. She found that all the emphasis on separate Black History and Black Culture courses in Highland Park did not prepare her for basic college studies. Besides that, Kalamazoo College suffers from many of the same attitudes we have in Highland Park.

Negro students maintain self-imposed segregation and ostracize their former friends who socialize with whites. LuJuan said she began to feel like a zombie, belonging in neither world.

We checked into both parochial schools and Cass Tech High School, a Detroit school once reputed for its scholastic achievement, but found neither suitable for our needs. A February, 1973 article in *Time* magazine gave national attention to the increasingly worsening conditions at Cass Tech, which takes only top-level students from all of the Detroit high schools. The overcrowded conditions, lack of space, and inability to secure the building from outsiders are only some of the problems there.

I cannot deny that our children could receive a better education elsewhere. But it is my feeling that we *do* have to suffer through the consequences of a poorer educational system. If all those who can afford to move or send their children to other schools, do so, then what is to happen to the majority of Negro children who must, by necessity, remain in the lower-achieving schools? We have to work *within* the school system to bring it up to par. The exodus of the more affluent and well-educated people to areas far from the cities is a major problem confronting us today. The city has become the hole in the doughnut and the situation is getting worse as it feeds upon itself.

The bright, motivated Negro students are desperately needed in the ghetto schools. Only they can set the standard of excellence against which all students should measure themselves. Only these students can motivate their peers to strive for academic goals as well as athletic achievements. They know education means fulfillment and a chance to make it; thousands of deprived young Negroes must learn educational standards spell freedom from ignorance and poverty, not just another form of white-imposed discrimination designed to prevent us Americans from improving our lot.

This is a very difficult question facing parents today, particularly in the Detroit area where the issue of busing school children to achieve integration is still to be decided

119

by the courts. In anticipation of the outcome, people are already fleeing the city. Even the most liberal of integrationists are concerned about the quality of education for their children if the court decides that the suburbs must integrate with the Detroit schools. If this is what is necessary to have an integrated society with concerned parents and, hopefully, better schools in the future, then I'm all for it, even if it temporarily means a setback for our own children. We have to take a long-range view.

Many Negroes, of course, do not agree with me; some, incidentally cultivate a separate Negro school system. Such is the case in Highland Park. At the city council meetings, which I sometimes attend in conjunction with my job as Deputy Administrator for the Community Development Department, I met councilmen who *wanted* the city to be all Black. They wanted only Black administrators in the schools and Black doctors in this hospital. (Anne is now Personnel Director at Highland Park Hospital).

In Highland Park in 1973 we've had to deal with a recall campaign against Mayor Robert B. Blackwell. These same people who want an all-black city want a new all-black mayor who will cater to their black demands and be in favor of reverse discrimination. What we have at the moment is an honest Negro mayor who is for equal rights for everyone, not just for the majority.

Another example of today's problem is an incident I was involved in that went to court. During a committee meeting in which we were listening to a white employee report, a so-called "black" councilman, Councilman Jesse P. Miller, disrupted the proceedings. He said he wanted a "black man" in place of the "white" employee who was an expert on the problem we were discussing. I simply told my fellow employee to pack up and go home, and I called the meeting for another time. As I was leaving, this councilman began shouting at me and calling me slanderous, obscene names. *While in the hall he called me a "mother-fucker and a son-of-a-bitch . . ."*

We took him to court and were disappointed that the case was "dismissed" on a technicality that Miller's attorney testified his client was not properly notified to appear. What disappointed us even more was what the "Negro" Judge, Donald L. Hobson, said to the attorneys later in his chambers concerning the obscene names I was called that they were "common, accepted language, *especially among black people.*"

Each time these councilmen talk about their black city and their soul brothers, their fifteen-or-so cohorts in the city council's audience applaud these notions. As per usual, it is the more militant and exploitive Negroes who attend these meetings and make their views known. By no means, however, do they speak for the majority of Negroes. The old familiar specter of hatred between the races is a dramatic example of the ills which, tragically, combine some of the most insoluble problems of a large city and a small suburb in a city-suburb that could not hope to gain enough control of its own surroundings to achieve the self-determination its more vocal citizens seek.

I have no "soul brothers" who are involved in the separation of America or its citizens. Each person deserves my respect because of what he is, not because of the color of his skin. I thoroughly agree with such writers as syndicated columnist Carl T. Rowan who suggest that we do not need this kind of "Black solidarity." In an article on February 5, 1973, in the *Detroit News,* titled, "Black Pride: Hair's Not Where It's At," he suggests that it's nonsense to follow these Black-pride fads and assume it is the epitome of pride in racial heritage. The dress, the hair, the mannerisms of speech are not going to reflect "meaningful black pride until more black people are making solid achievements in competition with the white majority. Nothing galls me more than a black dude who is cutting classes, or who never reads a newspaper, magazine, or book, or who won't hold onto a job, or who won't give a dime to some needy black, sitting around the barbershop or the pool hall or the student union, talking about how his "rags" or his "fro" symbolize black pride. . . . A lot of young people think they are snowing whitey. They are going through his university, taking his degree,

121

without submitting to the rigors of his academic prcedures. . . . These young blacks are snowing themselves."

Let there be no mistake, we need, indeed it is necessary to have, pride in ourselves, our background and our heritage, but not for the sake of blackness itself. We must see beyond the color of a man's skin. Too often, we are mistaking the appearance of pride for the real thing.

It will serve us all to run our city governments honestly and fairly for everyone. The flight to the suburbs has left a Negro majority holding the reins. We have to try to stand behind our cities and uphold principles of democracy, justice, and decency, regardless of whether our predecessors did so. This is the only way we can fight decay in public safety and in our educational system.

I involved myself in a fight in Highland Park to end another form of corruption. Our city charter states that a councilman is to receive $4,000 a year salary for parttime work and the council president to receive $4,500 *with no other compensation.* But the city has also been supplying these people with a new automobile and free gas which most have been using for their regular jobs and personal convenience. When the cars are a year old they are sold. The council recently passed an ordinance granting *them* the first preference to purchase the cars assigned to them—then to put them on competitive sale to the highest bidder. This ordinance action is illegal.

This kind of graft hurts all the citizens. However, I have been attacked by those who benefit from this "special privilege;" they seem to think I am being disloyal for uncovering something which defies our city laws.

At a time when views such as this are not the most vocal ones, when those of us who hold these views are subject to ridicule by militants and separatists, one has to wonder if a lifelong dedication to this idea has been worthwhile. Now, in 1973, Anne and our children want to return to California where our former house still waits for us and where, for once in our lives, we can relax. This was not our thinking when we made the move to Michigan, but being engulfed with such racial bitterness, with the busing issue and the middle class

122

"white Irene McCabe-type exploitation" being so rampant, we want now to emphasize our family relationships to a greater extent than our community involvement allowed us in the past. Only once in our married life have we taken a real solid family vacation. In 1969 we took the children in our car and in six weeks time we visited every state in the nation with the exception of Alaska, Hawaii, and New Hampshire. That vacation epitomizes our life. Rushing, we've tried to do a lot in a short time. Now Anne says, "I'm fifty years old. You're seventy, though you may look and act only forty. Back in our early married years, I always thought that the next few years would bring relaxation and peace and a time to ourselves. It never has. Now, we have to be a little bit selfish and consider our own family ahead of others for a change. Our eight children need us, particularly those still at home. Our youngest is ten years old and still has a lot of growing up to do."

And LuJuan, my eighteen-year-old daughter who is a college freshman, would prefer to put on her college forms that she is an Indian, rather than a Negro (my mother's Indian background). Given a preference, as she is because of her light skin and varied racial background (Anne's father is white), LuJuan does not really wish to associate herself with the "ugly American" stigma of being black-white or black-white-black. In explaining to her that we can alter some Negroes' attitudes by trying to effect changes from within the Negro race, I met with a challenge. She asked, "Daddy, what good has this turmoil all your life done? You've been working to change people all these years. Has anything really been accomplished?"

The latter question is one I've had to consider very seriously ever since I decided I was not going to accept the status quo and at every juncture in my life since then. The security trial, the court suits, the constant fight for integration have been taxing. Existentialist that I am, I have to leave some impression in this world; I have to try to make an impact; I have to fight for what I believe in.

The battles against racial hatred have been fought and

123

won and then fought again all my life. LuJuan is right on that point. But maybe what she and others like her should consider is that repetition is the essence of discrimination; racial bias can be likened to a cookie cutter which is stamped onto each new life situation in which a so-called black person finds himself. The imprint of the cookie cutter can be changed, but the frustration remains that racial discrimination stereotypes the events in our lives and forces us to reshape their stifling, narrow confines always almost as though for the first time. The process becomes only imperceptibly easier and considerably more discouraging with each successive encounter. The hard truth is that all the progress the civil right movement has made for my lifetime has been achieved so gradually it was often mistaken for stagnation. I try to explain to LuJuan—it didn't just happen today.

What we have achieved so far is forty hours a week integration. As you can see in many instances by the city of Highland Park, we work together from eight until five, but we return to our separate neighborhoods and separate church and social gatherings. There is so much more left to fight for.

When we left California, we promised our children that they could return there and attend college and live in their former home. I know now that we'll be leaving Highland Park and going back to permanently settle in California sometime in the not-too-distant future, but I won't be going back to a tranquil life of warm sunshine and palm trees. Even now, there's a bitter move among the dominant militant group in San Bernardino to maintain control of community affairs. I plan to continue the fight. I wouldn't have it any other way.

A majority of Americans who are thinking, and are well aware of what is really happening, will not allow other Americans to place us in verbal segregation by the overt use of race as "black." This is evidenced by Ossie Davis, the movie director, and his wife, Ruby Dee, who spoke at New York State University at Buffalo. Both emphasized that certain movies created for Negro audiences were pure exploitation and should be left unseen. Mr. Davis said movie goers should shun movies such as "Superfly" and "The

124

Mack." ". . . We're making pimps heroes. We've got to stop this nonsense . . . such films are making phenomenal amounts of money . . . we're paying for images of our own degredation." Miss Dee stated: "Fascism is creeping into black films. . . ."

So the Negro is now "progressing" from the stereotyped watermelon eating, banjo plucking, chicken stealing character to the "Modern Black Mafia," dope baron and gun slinger. This is not true and images so depicted are only reflected in the eyes of those Americans who wish it so and they are a minority of a very few.

The stereotype of the "black pimp hero" is also reflected in Judge Hobson's remark about obscene language. Most Negroes do not use obscene terms in general or normal conversation anymore than other groups, and it is a minority which is giving the rest of us this image, through the black exploitation films and through the behavior and appearance of some older as well as young people. This gangster image should be realized for what it represents overall, a very, very few people.

Our system of "Checks and Balances" has prevailed and always will—Sobeit in these United States.

CHAPTER NINE

THIRTY-FOUR YEARS,
THREE WARS AND SIX MONTHS LATER . . .
"CHEHAW" AND TUSKEGEE, ALABAMA

IN PRECEDING CHAPTERS I RELATED TO MY AS-
signment and work in the Tuskegee Army Air Force Sub-
Depot, Tuskegee Institute, Alabama. The railroad station
there, "Chehaw," became a byword of many meanings to
many military and civilian personnel of World War II who
were assigned or served, even briefly, at the Tuskegee Sub-
Depot, Moton Field. It seemed natural and appropriate
in many minds and attitudes of the nineteen seventies re-
verting to the nostalgia of people, places and things, much in
common, that the alumnae and alumni of "Chehaw"—Tuskegee, Alabama—would join in efforts to have a reunion.

On August 11, 12 and 13, 1972 Tuskegee Airmen came
from far and near to meet in Detroit, Michigan to reminisce,
exchanging and documenting many experiences and incidents of the 1940-1950 years . . . and also to share in silence
a tribute of gratitude, respect and honor to their comrades
who had to fight their way out of America . . . to fight for
America . . . in Africa, Europe, Asia . . . and America. We
who survived now knew the true meaning of "CHEHAW"
. . . this was no Armageddon . . . no Plain of Megiddo . . .

126

and no war to end all wars. Our comrades we honored in silent prayer were like our fathers who fought and died in France in World War I . . . their fathers who fought and died in the battle of San Juan Hill . . . and their fathers who fought and died in the battle of Gettysburg and many other battles of the Civil War, all who served . . . "that those who died did not die in vain."

We remembered those who defied and defiled the perfecting of our democracy by exploiting race, religion, color and national origin . . . Senators Theodore Bilbo, James Eastland and Herman Talmadge, Sr., demagogues with racial slurs and false statements in U.S. Congress. Senator Joseph McCarthy's all-out efforts in the malicious destruction of characters and reputations by his innuendos and false charges of subversive activities. George C. Wallace and Orville Faubus demagoguery and defiance against education. Bull Connors, Lester Maddox, Rap Brown, Irene McCabe, Stokely Carmichael, Ku Klux Klan, White Citizens Council, Black Panthers and the "DAP"—organizations of extremist bigots and racists, just to name a few. As I look back into these and other such exploiters and exploiting groups, they have been milestones in improving and perfecting the American system and its democracy, although it was certainly not their intent and purpose. The bigotry and demagoguery was so violent and undermining it made the majority of decent Americans see the need and importance of equality and human rights for their fellow man.

This Tuskegee Airmen's reunion in 1972 was so successful the group formed into a tentative national organization and elected officers and a governing board. They decided that instead of an annual reunion they would combine and hold annual conventions every year on August 2, 3, and 4. They met in Washington, D.C. in 1973 and began the first all-out organization implementation. In 1974 they met in Los Angeles, California; each year the attendance increased from the beginning in Detroit of two hundred fifty ex-airmen to the Los Angeles convention of well over six hundred, and their wives and families swelled the number more than double. In Los Angeles the Tuskegee Airmen became of age. They elected permanent national officers, established three regional sections, Eastern, Central and Western regions, with local Chapters, such as the Detroit Chapter, Washington Chapter, Los Angeles Chapter, Chicago Chapter, and others.

I am a member of the Detroit Chapter of the Tuskegee Airmen, and in April 1973 we were invited by officials of the U.S. Air Force, Dayton, Ohio, to attend the dedication ceremonies of the long overdue and ignored record of the Americans who trained and served at Tuskegee Sub-Depot during World War II. We found it to be not only a segregated exhibit by spot placement in the museum building, but also designated in terms of race and color. Of course as usual there were those few minority group members who were color or race oriented that wanted the exhibit segregated and designated as "black Airmen."

The Detroit Chapter opposed the use of race and color, and insisted the exhibit be integrated as were all the other exhibits and let the eyes and mind of the beholder determine, if they must, race or color. The Detroit Chapter's preference was not "black Airmen" but Tuskegee Airmen. Again it was a necessary matter of being proud to be Americans in America. Approximately sixteen months after stating our objectives, writing several well placed letters and making several top official contacts, Lloyd "Scotty" Hathcock, Sr., a member of the Dayton Tuskegee Airmen, informed us that the Air Force Museum had dismantled the exhibit and was integrating our participation as airmen in World War II within the exact periods and phases as were other historical Air Force exhibits. Scotty said, ". . . we will be designated as 'Tuskegee Airmen' and all references of color and race are to be eliminated except as one sees it."

Contemptuously some so-called white Americans have often referred to other Americans as "spooks," so as a matter of "private" jest and a "throw-out" during World War II, Tuskegee Airmen dubbed themselves as "The Spookwaffe"—a play on words to the German air force "Luftwaffe." However, these Tuskegee Airmen established such an enviable record that the reference "The Spookwaffe" stuck and became commonplace in public knowledge. It was accepted openly with the highest degree of dignity and honor.

A report written by the 332d's commander, General B.O. Davis in a report, December 1944 stated, "I cannot fail to mention the all-important fact that your achievements have been recognized. Unofficially you are known by an untold number of bomber crews as the "Red Tails" (the markings on their fighter planes' tail surfaces were painted red) who can be depended upon and whose appearance means certain protection from enemy bombers. The bomber crews have told others about your accomplishments, and your good reputation has preceded you in many parts where you may think you are unknown. . . . The Commanding General of our fighter Command has stated that we are doing a good job and that he will so inform the Air Force Commander. Thus the official report of our operations is a creditable one."

"The Spookwaffe" is officially credited with shooting down more German planes over Anzio than any other fighter squadron in the history of World War II. President Harry S. Truman awarded, to the Tuskegee Airmen, the Presidential Unit Citation for the unsurpassed record of destroying eighty-two enemy aircraft in one day. During all escort missions in the 15th Air Force under the command of Major General Nathan F. Twining they never lost a plane.

On September 27, 1974, the Tuskegee Airman throughout the nation received an invitation from Major Johnny L. Ford inviting us to attend dedication ceremonies at Moton Field in Tuskegee, Alabama.

Nostalgia, yes, this was of the yesteryear . . . thirty-four years in the past, an invitation to return to our own "Meadow of Honor" . . . the hallowed grounds of Tuskegee Sub-Depot and see the "Chehaw" station . . . flashbacks in memories . . . where we did as Sterling A. Brown wrote, "Strong men keep acomin' on . . ." It was there in Alabama we proved ourselves inch by inch against strong and vicious odds, our loyalty, determination and allegiance to America. It was there in Alabama, where approximately twenty-two years later, George C. Wallace stood in the door of the University of Alabama, representing the highest office of the state and white supremacy, making an all-out effort to bar Autherine Lucy from an education. It was there we wrote into the history of these United States, as our forefathers had done, that our contributions and investment in this land are second to none.

Wardell Polk, Alexander Jefferson, Bill Goode, Wentz Perkins and I arrived in Tuskegee, Alabama Thursday morning, October 3 at nine o'clock. We registered at the Holiday Inn and were having breakfast when Barbara Williams and Alberta Simons met us in the dining room. They lived in Tuskegee and Jeff had called Barbara and Alberta, who were closely connected with Tuskegee community activities, to let them know we had arrived. They arranged to take us on a bus tour to Chehaw and the old Air Base area. As we were waiting for the bus we were joined by Della Raney, the first nurse assigned to Tuskegee Sub-Depot, Bill Womack, both from Detroit, and Lloyd "Scotty" Hathcock from Dayton, Ohio, and a number of other Tuskegee Airmen from other Chapters throughout the nation. They had all arrived by air that morning.

We first visited the Chehaw railroad station, which had public notices posted on it stating that it was to be demolished and removed. The platforms and surrounding area were used as a log loading site. The doors leading to the passenger waiting rooms were removed or open. All of us looked for the "colored" and "white" signs and other specific items as souvenirs. Someone had beaten us to them, so we rummaged through old papers, etc., on the floor.

As we were making pictures in and around the station, a large diesel engine came into the area with quite a handsome and congenial dark brown-skinned engineer at the controls. He and his crew of three, one a blond blue-eyed brakeman, took several minutes from their duties and schedule to pose with us in making pictures. Wardell Polk said, ". . . this is a long way up from 1942 and station masters' or train conductors' approach of, '. . . boy what ch'all want?' . . ."

We next went to the old Tuskegee Sub-Depot area and even though all the buildings were demolished and removed

130

many years ago, we did find the runways that were almost overgrown with high grass. The weeds and trees completely covered what we had known as streets and parade grounds . . . we recounted, recreated, and stood for several minutes in silence to our fellow Americans, who died in the cause of freedom and democracy on this land and foreign lands. There were moist hearts and eyes among us. The mind does reflect in strange ways, during those moments of silence. I remembered being in Dunbar High School, in Lynchburg, Virginia, in 1922, while Professor J. A. Jordan was directing a chorus group to sing the Recessional . . . "The tumult and the shouting dies—the captains and the kings depart—still stands thine ancient sacrifice, an humble and a contrite heart—Lord God of hosts, be with us yet, lest we forget—lest we forget." It was most appropriate . . . here.

We boarded the bus and drove to the old flight area. At the far end of the runway we noted several people and a station wagon. The station wagon was from the National Broadcasting Company television. There were two TV camera crewmen, an attractive brownskinned girl and retired General Noel F. Parrish. During World War II Noel Parish was commanding officer at Tuskegee Sub-Depot. We were happy to see him; he had attended all three of our prior reunions and conventions but we were not aware that he was attending this dedication. It was a noisy "old hometown type" meeting.

The brownskinned girl immediately stepped in, and without identifying herself, made known her badge of authority very forcefully, school mom fashion. "I am doing a television program and you are interferring. If you stand back and stay absolutely quiet you can remain; but there will be no further interruptions . . ." This was her first big mistake. The next one was when she reached to the mouth of one of the blond cameramen, extracted a cigarette, took several puffs from it, then placed it back between his lips again. She blew the smoke from her mouth and also "blew" whatever image of poise and dignity she had left. Here was a girl who was in her twenties or thirties displaying that she was "Miss NBC" in 1974, and not realizing the fact that tact, good judgment and a better choice of words and actions could have added to the entire picture, of full acceptance, to these men who had thirty years before her existence stood on these grounds. . . .

Her name was Janie Taylor. Ironically her father, Edward Taylor, was also a Tuskegee Airman, a member of the 332nd group; in part, that is how she was assigned this project. She was from a Washington, D.C. NBC station, WRC-TV News Center Channel 4, and was requested on this assignment by the Washington Tuskegee Airmen's Chapter. Wardell Polk asked her what was the purpose of her program and she replied curtly, reaching for the cigarette again, "I am here to get a story of the Tuskegee Airmen and I am getting it from General Parish." Wardell stated, "That's great, but since we are here, and with all due respect to General Parish, who was incidental to our being, you should agree that we were the overall group and were the major subjects of the Tuskegee Airmen; so why overlook this representative group?"

"Miss NBC's" reply was cold and bitter: "You can't structure my story for me. My father was a member of the 332nd group which was a part of the Tuskegee Airmen and he has given me all that is necessary . . ." I interrupted her and asked, "Did your father give you the background of how they were included within the Air Corps? Are you aware that President Harry Truman played a major role in the Tuskegee story, prior to his becoming President, along with Mary McLeod Bethune, Eleanor Roosevelt, Edgar Brown, A. Phillip Randolph, Governor Dwight H. Green of Illinois and others? Did you know that the first money to sponsor a flight to Washington, D.C., in 1939 to meet a Congressional Committee asking that we be included in flight training programs was given by the Jones Brothers of Chicago?"

Miss Taylor's expression was one of absolute frustration and confusion. She looked at her co-worker NBC crew for aid, then at General Parrish. Nobody came to her rescue. However, she did reply, "I've said I know what I want and all of that is irrelevant and has nothing to do with what was here." As she turned away I said, "This certainly sounds like old times; maybe the dialogue is not exact but the ring is the same as some thirty years ago and the 'great white father' and types like you made 'Chehaw' a well understood meaning. Somehow I know you may not understand what I am saying when I say, 'Nothing has changed, John Brown, nothing has changed.' But sometime in the near future you will know exactly what I am saying and exactly what we mean."

Janie Taylor was boiling inside—she got the message; and it was clearly evident. She turned abruptly away and said, "General, we'll continue;" and that they did. Our group loaded into the bus and, aside from several uncomplimentary remarks about her, we left the area. My mind flashed back to another incident I had had with another NBC employee in 1950, WLW-TV, Cincinnati, Ohio. His name was Neil Van Els.

My wife and I had met "Judy King" who was Major General Ben I. Funk's wife. Mrs. Funk was the producer of a local variety television show under her professional name —"The Judy King Show"—through WLW-TV. We introduced a very talented young couple, Robert and Roberta Alexander, to Mrs. Funk. She auditioned them and presented them on her show. They sang several songs from *Porgy and Bess* that received a great amount of public response. A local merchant was interested in sponsoring them to appear on a fifteen minute television spot, but Neil Van Els told him they did not belong to the union (American Guild of Variety Artists or the Musicians Union). Anne and I tried several contacts and success looked possible until Neil Van Els called me at my home and told me I was not a certified or licensed agent; so our next effort was to obtain an agent.

Ironically, we were directed to an agent by one of the "McGuire Sisters," who I was told later married Neil Van Els. They were not together too long before they separated. Anne and I were almost successful in meeting all demands and requirements necessary for Bob and Berts performing on television for the "Parkmoor" commercial and show when the head of the then Negro musicians union came by

133

our home and informed me that, ". . . Mr. Van Els can make trouble for our union as well as for me if I let your friends go on, and particularly since they are newcomers to Ohio. They will have to live here for a year before I can give them a union card and OK them to appear."

I said, "You have given them a union card and work permit and they have paid the fee." He replied, "Yes; but I did not know they had been here such a short time." Bob interrupted and said, "I told you when I first met you I had been teaching music in a high school in Virginia and resigned in June to come to Dayton to work for the Air Force" —the union head interrupted, "Bob, you know how it is to have to get along with Mr. Van Els, and his folks can really make things tough for us. . . . I'll let you keep your union card and you can appear at any clubs and top spots in the area; I'll help you and we'll let this issue cool off, 'cause Van Els is mad . . ."

So Bob appeared at a local night club and accepted his job as a civilian employee at Headquarters, Air Materiel Command, Wright-Patterson Air Force Base, Ohio. Shortly thereafter Neil Van Els was transferred to a higher position with the National Broadcasting Company in New York . . . so, "John Brown, nothing has really changed, nothing has really changed. . . ."

Shortly after Mayor Coleman Young entered his office as Mayor of Detroit he made a classic statement; he said, "These people ain't giving up their hold on this city easy." Mayor Young is a Tuskegee Airman and a member of the Detroit Chapter. While we were in Los Angeles at the convention Wardell and I were having breakfast with the Mayor and we began talking over several isues of current news, etc. Wardell mentioned Mayor Young's statement and I added, ". . . a helluva lot of 'those other' people are making it easy for Coleman's 'these people' to hold on by being exponents of a strictly black-for-black cause and then trying to 'out-black each other.' "

Our group had just witnessed and left the NBC-Janie Taylor-Tuskegee Airmen incident of Chehaw when we decided to stop by Mayor Johnny Ford's office in Tuskegee.

We entered and were greeted by his Administrative Assistant, Mildred Moore. Mayor Ford was not in so we talked for quite a while with Ms. Moore and other City officials in the office about our trip down to Alabama and thirty-four years after World War II, until I said, ". . . I remember many things about my 1940 assignment at Tuskegee and even long after those years I remember the George C. Wallace, the Governor of Alabama who rode the reins of white supremacy to obtain his office. I can yet remember him standing in the doorway of the University of Alabama refusing to allow Autherine Lucy to enter and his challenging the U.S. Marshalls who were sent to escort her into the building, and raising the Confederate flag over the State Capitol in preference to the flag of these United States, in order to discourage the march on Selma and voter registration . . ."

Mildred Moore interrupted me and said, "It's too damn bad about Autherine Lucy! We think around here that Governor Wallace is alright in our book. A lot of good things that are happening in Tuskegee are happening because of the Governor. He was just here last week for a ground breaking ceremony and would be here today at this dedication of Moton Field but he has a prior commitment. He is giving Tuskegee quite a few million dollars. . . ."

I said, "Thank God he is not going to be here for the dedication scheduled today. Since Mayor Ford has been kind enough to invite me I certainly do not wish to offend or show him any disrespect by not attending the ceremonies in protest to George Wallace. To you and others who forget so much, so fast, so easy, I remind you and say what Sterling A. Brown has written: ". . . They bought off some of your leaders—you stumbled, as blind men will . . . they coaxed you unwontedly soft voiced . . . you followed a way. Then laughed as usual. They heard the laugh and wondered; uncomfortable; unadmitting a deeper terror. . . . The strong men keep a-comin' on—gittin' stronger."

I bowed deep to Mildred Moore; she looked at me perplexed. I kissed her hand and backed away, the entire group laughed—even the Chief of Police who was also in

135

the office. Ms. Moore smiled and suggested we wait in Mayor Ford's office. We waited for Mayor Ford in his office and enjoyed ourselves reading and discussing the many mementos and curios on the walls and on tables in the room. We were soon joined by Mayor Ford and Lou Rawls.

In April, 1975 George Wallace, Jr. was a guest on the ToDay television morning program to present his book *The Wallaces of Alabama*. During the interview Jim Hartz asked young George Wallace about his father's infamous statement, ". . . Segregation Now! Segregation Tomorrow! Segregation Forever!" Young George Wallace replied that George Wallace, Sr. had never had any racial feelings or attitudes against any group or race of people. And that the governor's stand against Autherine Lucy in the doorway of the University of Alabama was only a test of a Constitutional question of law. As I looked closely at the facial expression, on this young man being interviewed before a vast television audience, to me the look on his face did not communicate the same thing that his words just expressed. He knew his father had been elected on a racist platform and he had just lied.

Wallace used the issue of race much of his political career, toward and into the office as governor. Not only for himself, but when he could not succeed himself as governor of the State of Alabama, he used his image and appeal to elect his wife, Lurleen Wallace, as governor in order to return to the governor's office after her term expired. Lurleen Wallace was elected and George Wallace became governor again after her term ended.

In 1963 George Corley Wallace campaigned and repeatedly promised to personally stand and block the door of any white Alabama school to keep any Negro children from entering. As he delivered his inaugural address for this third term of office as governor, he finished with his inciting and inflammatory statement:

". . . In the name of the greatest people that have ever trod on this earth, I draw the line in the dust and toss the gauntlet before the feet of tyranny. And I say: Segregation Now! Segregation Tomorrow! Segregation Forever!" The white citizens were jubilant, they gave the rebel yell and joyous screams with a long lasting ovation.

Twelve years later during my return trip to Alabama I met an Alabama citizen who heard Wallace's inaugural speech and she said she listened because she thought Lurleen Wallace's tragic death from cancer had softened him in his thinking—then Alberta said, "His closing speech statement—'. . . Segregation Now! Segregation Tomorrow! Segregation Forever!' typifies a demagogue, a racist and a tyrant. NOW, TOMORROW and FOREVER. After he was shot and crippled, I felt sorrow and hurt for him—but now, Chauncey, the real Wallace is covered; he's gone underground. He wants to be President. We cannot afford to be sorry for him. He's left too much hatred and 'unAmerican' in America—his acts and statements of violence and hatred will live for a long time."

If we are going to be Americans, for God's sake, for freedom, for justice, for a true democracy, we cannot allow nor ever forget leaders who have exploited the goodness of the American people. Wallace has fostered and fomented that disastrous prejudice which has become the major factor in our country's dissension.

The Jews did not nor will not ever forget . . . Americans should not ever forget!

TUSKEGEE AIRMEN—"IT HAPPENED THIS WAY"

Currently little is known, prior to the activation of the 99th Pursuit Squadron on 22 March 1941 at Tuskegee Sub-Depot, Alabama, of the so called black Americans' interest and participation in aviation.

The Tuskegee Airmen, a national organization composed of civilian and military personnel of World War II, made a concerted effort to research and document, for historical and public information, the beginning and background of their predecessors and their contributions to the current inclusion of all Americans within the United States Air Force of today.

Almost from the very beginning of aviation in the United States of America, so called black Americans have been interested and shown concern in aviation. Paul Lawrence Dunbar, (1872-1906) American poet and novelist, in Dayton, Ohio, was a close friend and associate of Orville and Wilbur Wright who built and flew the first successful heavier-than-air machine.

Bessie Coleman, a daring lady lion tamer and blues singer, was killed in Florida during the 1910-1920 period in an airplane crash, while taking flight instructions.

Eugene Bullard of Columbus, Georgia served during World War I in France with the French Foreign Legion and transferred to the French Air Service, November 15, 1916. After learning to fly he was assigned to a French Fighter Squadron as a pilot and was decorated with the Croix de Guerre with a star for his achievement record in aviation combat.

In 1928, Charles Alfred "Chief" Anderson of Bryn Mawr, Pennsylvania, bought an airplane for $3,000, and was given flight instruction at an airport near his home. White instructors, with very few exceptions, would not teach Negroes to fly unless the student would purchase his own airplane.

Charles Anderson purchased his own airplane in 1928 and paid $10.00 an hour flying time fee to his instructor. Four years later, in 1932, he had qualified and earned his commercial pilot's certificate—and according to all available records—he was the first Negro to qualify. "Chief" Anderson estimates the small piece of paper referred to as a "certificate" cost him, including the price of his aircraft, well over $6,000. Charles Anderson and Doctor Ernest Forsythe made a cross country flight that created national interest and was highly publicized in 1930.

Hubert Julian of New York and John C. Robinson of Chicago aroused added interest when they flew for Emperor, "The Lion of Juda," Haile Selassie during the Ethiopian-Italian conflict in 1936.

From the years 1936-1941 there were seven Negro aviators who had earned commercial pilot's certificates under the United States Civil Aeronautics Administration, they were:

Commercial Pilots—(7)

License #

7638—Charles A. Anderson, Bryn Mawr, Penn.
15897—John W. Greene, Jr., Boston, Mass.
29452—Robert Terry, Besking Ridge, New Jersey
32546—Earl W. Renfro, Chicago, Ill.
32630—George W. Allen, Latrobe, Penn.
36609—Cornelius R. Coffey, Oaklawn, Chicago, Ill.
54573—Charles M. Ashe, Philadelphia, Penn.

Limited Commercial Pilots—(2)
40217—Grover C. Nash, Chicago, Ill.
43814—Willa Beatrice Brown—Chicago, Ill.

There were 102 licensed Private Pilots and 160 licensed solo-student Pilots.

In 1936 two of the above Commercial Pilots, Cornelius R. Coffey and Earl W. Renfroe, qualified and obtained their Civil Aeronautics Administration Instructor's Rating as flight instructors. They gave flight instructions from the Harlem Airport located at 87th and Harlem Avenues, Oaklawn, Illinois. Willa Beatrice Brown also flew from Harlem Airport and it was Willa Brown who organized the first group of flyers for flight and aircraft mechanical instructions. She was energetic and attracted the attention of Enoc P. Waters, Jr. the City Editor of the *Chicago Defender*. He became interested in the efforts made by the group and told them of the possible advantages and opportunities they would have if they would merge their efforts and form an incorporated organization (non-profit). He would give them public exposure through the *Chicago Defender* with its publisher Robert S. Abbott's sponsorship and endorsement.

The first meeting, as were many others, was held at the Wabash Avenue Y.M.C.A. The original twelve members named the organization The National Airmen's Association of America with the post office address at the *Chicago Defender's* office, 3435 S. Indiana Avenue. With the full support of Robert Abbott, the knowhow and untiring effective efforts of Enoc P. Waters, and the efficient secretarial and punctual follow-up work of Willa Brown, contacts were made with top city, state, and national representatives. Air shows and exhibits were arranged that aroused public interest and participation.

The objective for which the National Airmen's Association of America was formed was, ". . . to further stimulate interest in aviation, and to bring about a better understanding in the entire field of aeronautics." With this basic aim and determination the NAAA decided in May, 1939, they would send representatives on a flight across the United

States to visit Negro colleges and universities to create interest and inform faculties and students of the National Airmen's Association of America's appeal to the United States government, Federal officials in Administration and Congress, that as American citizens Negroes be included in aviation training programs. Enoc Waters suggested that it would also be important that the two flyers representing the NAAA visit named congressional representatives in Washington, D.C., who would be contacted personally by top city and state officials of Illinois.

Contacts were made through the *Chicago Defender* by Mayor Edward J. Kelley of Chicago and Governor Dwight H. Green of Illinois with Senators James Slattery and Edward Dirksen to meet with flyers Dale L. White and Chauncey E. Spencer, of the NAAA, and Edgar G. Brown, President of the Government Employees Union in Washington, D.C. Mr. Brown was a personal friend of Enoc Waters who knew his way around Washington with many politicians. During one of his appearances before a congressional committe for the NAAA, Mr. Brown was so eloquent and articulate that *Time* magazine dubbed him as ". . . the silver tongued orator."

All plans with the schools to be visited and Washington contacts were completed for the two NAAA flyers to fly from Harlem Airport the first two weeks in May, 1939.

Spencer and White were both working on Works Progress Administration projects. Spencer had saved approximately five hundred dollars for the flight. This was just the amount needed to rent the airplane from a flyer at the airport, Art LaToure, who owned the Lincoln-Paige biplane. The NAAA made many efforts locally in order to raise more money to finance the flight but the answer in all instances was almost the same—that "the mission was foolhardy and foolish."

Spencer was working under Horace C. Cayton on a federal project gathering material and information for the publication of *Black Metropolis* and he mentioned to a co-worker, Queenie Davis, that they had run into a setback on their finances for the cross-country flight. Queenie suggested

141

that she had friends, the Jones Brothers, Ed and George, who then headed the number policy in Chicago and also owned the Ben Franklin Department store on 47th Street. She would see whether they would help. Queenie did arrange a meeting. Enoc Waters, Spencer, and White met with Mr. Edward P. Jones and came away with one thousand dollars. Spencer and White flew from Harlem Airport as planned May 9, 1939 in a Lincoln-Paige biplane. Approximately three hours later they were forced down in a farmer's back yard in Sherwood, Ohio with a broken crankshaft. It took them two days and one night to repair the damages and resume their flight to the schools and into Washington. However, they were grounded temporarily in Pittsburgh for landing at the Allegheny Airport, at night with no lights, behind a commercial airliner.

The next morning the CAA Inspector cleared them to resume their flight on to Washington when he, Inspector Goff, learned that they were forced to fly into Pittsburgh because the Morgantown, West Virginia Airport was under construction and had no place to store their plane. They were met at the Pittsburgh-Allegheny Airport by staff members of the *Pittsburgh Courier*—William G. Nunn, Sr. and Chester L. Washington. The publisher of the *Pittsburgh Courier,* attorney Robert L. Vann, gave Spencer and White five hundred dollars and letters to influential representatives in Washington. Spencer and White flew directly from Pittsburgh to Washington, D.C.

Edgar Brown and members of the Negro press met the flyers at the Washington Airport. They had conferences with a number of officials who promised their support. At the time a little noted incident actually was the turning point and most important incident of the entire trip. As they departed from the electric car that runs underground to the Congressional building, Edgar Brown stopped and greeted a man he addressed as Senator. He introduced Spencer and White to him as Senator Harry Truman and explained that they had flown to Washington from Chicago in their airplane to try to get the Arms Appropriation Committee to apropriate a special amount of money in order that the Negro be included in the Civilian Pilot Training Program. Mr. Truman showed immediate surprise that Negroes were not included in the proposed training and a greater surprise that the Air Corps did not admit Negroes. He wanted to see the airplane they flew to Washington and arranged to come to the airport that afternoon.

Senator Truman met Mr. Brown and the flyers at the airport and asked many questions. Upon leaving he said to Spencer and White, ". . . if you had guts enough to fly this thing to Washington . . . I've got guts enough to see that you get what you are asking for. . . ."

True to his word Senator Truman directed his efforts to President Franklin D. Roosevelt and joined with Mrs. Eleanor Roosevelt, Mrs. Mary McLeod Bethune, Edgar Brown, Secretary of War Robert H. Hinckley, Congressmen Arthur W. Mitchell, J. Hamilton Lewis, Everett Dirksen, Emmett O'Neil, James Slattery, and the Negro press, in asking President Roosevelt and Congress that provisions be made which would guarantee Negro inclusion and full participation in both the Civilian Pilot Training Program and the United States Air Corps.

President Roosevelt responded and outlined to Congress a national defense program. He stated, ". . . the changing world conditions outside the American hemisphere made it imperative for the United States to take immediate steps for the protection of the liberties and pursuits of all its citizens."

The Seventy-Sixth Congress inserted a clause in Section 4 of H.R. Bill 3791 which read: "The Secretary of War is hereby authorized .. . to lend to accredited civilian aviation schools one or more of which shall be designated by the CAA (Civilian Aviation Authority) for the training of Negro Air Pilots."

Spencer and White returned to Chicago after visiting the colleges and universities. The cross-country flight was a greater success than planned. Inquiries from schools, students, and governmental agencies and representatives were many. The NAAA was formed as a non-profit corporation under the State of Illinois. Letters were sent from the NAAA

143

to all listed and known civilian pilots, and others interested in aviation, regarding a proposed plan to hold a conference in Chicago the third week in August, 1940. The responses were immediate and full of optimism. Pilots and aviation enthusiasts came to Chicago from all sections of the nation, and though they totaled small in number, approximately fifty-six pilots and thirty-eight others interested in the aims and objectives, the three day conference had to be extended to five to fully cover the overall program. The NAAA became a national functional and well organized body. The Negro press gave constant support and publicity. The organization maintained direct contacts with congressional representatives, state and national. The aims and objectives of the National Airmen's Association of America became a reality on the activation of the 99th Pursuit Squadron on March 22, 1941 at Tuskegee Sub-Depot, Tuskegee, Alabama.

Certain opposing forces within governmental agencies realized that the inclusion of the Negro into Civilian Pilot Training Program and the United States Air Corps was a reality. They centered their efforts to maintain patterns of absolute segregation.

West Virginia State College, Institute, West Virginia, was one of the first Negro Colleges which took active part in the Civilian Pilots Training Program. Other colleges included:

Tuskegee Institute, Tuskegee, Alabama
Hampton Institute, Hampton, Virginia
Howard University, Washington, D.C.
North Carolina Agricultural and Technical State University, Greensboro, North Carolina
Delaware State College, Dover, Delaware

There was a scattering of Negroes in many other schools throughout the country and two non-college units in the Chicago area. The latter two were also a direct result of the National Airmen's Association of America aims. It was operated by Willa Beatrice Brown and named the Coffey

School of Aeronautics. The Coffey School of Aeronautics was located at the Harlem Airport, Oak Lawn, Illinois and named for Cornelius Coffey, one of the nation's earliest certified flight instructors and President of the NAAA.

Opening his Senate re-election Campaign at Sedalia, Missouri, June 15, 1940, Senator Harry S. Truman said: "In giving Negroes the rights that are theirs, we are only acting in accord with our ideals of a true democracy." Mr. Truman remained consistent with the efforts of his office to implement the inclusion of Negroes within both flight training programs.

In 1940, A. Phillip Randolph, the President of the Brotherhood of Sleeping Car Porters, and President of the National Negro Congress, organized the first March on Washington to force the Roosevelt Administration to give equal opportunities of employment in government and industry holding federal contracts. The intended march never became a reality because President Roosevelt issued Executive Order 8802, which prohibited discrimination because of race, creed, color, religion or national origin. The Executive Order aplied to all federal agencies and/or industry that were working on federal contracts.

The 99th Pursuit Squadron was activated on 22 March 1941. Major General Walter R. Weaver delivered the inaugural address on the Tuskegee Campus in front of the Booker T. Washington Memorial. The 100th Squadron was activated on 19 February 1942. The first Tuskegee Airmen, a class of five, graduated from Tuskegee Air Base as commissioned officers and pilots in the United States Air Corps in July, 1942.

Discrimination and separation of races was a continued practice in military organizations. The Office of Civilian Aide to the Office of the Secretary of War was established to monitor and check acts of discrimination in the military service. Appointed to serve as civilian aides and assistant aides were:

The Honorable William H. Hastie	James C. Evans
Truman K. Gibson, Jr.	Louis Lautier

On 5 January 1943 after repeated acts of discrimination and open defiance by military officials of Executive Order 8802, Judge Wiliam H. Hastie informed the Secretary of War, Henry L. Stimson and Under Secretary Robert P. Patterson, that in the Air Forces, "further retrogression is now so apparent and recent occurrences are so objectionable and inexcusable that I have no alternative but to resign in protest and to give public expression to my views." Judge Hastie asked his assistants, Truman K. Gibson, Jr., James C. Evans, and Louis Lautier to stay at their posts as aides to the Secretary of War. The Associated Negro Press lauded Judge Hastie for his stand and statement in resigning and reported that "the consensus of opinion as expressed freely and frankly is that he did the right thing in stepping out of a position that was becoming untenable." Truman K. Gibson, Jr. was appointed acting civilian aide for seven months with Louis Lautier and James C. Evans his assistants.

President Franklin Roosevelt died April 12, 1945. On 9 April 1945 at Freeman Field, Seymour, Indiana, by Order of Colonel Robert R. Selway, Jr. United States Air Corps, one hundred and one (101) Negro commissioned officers were ordered by Base Regulation number 85-2 to use "separate housing, messing, recreational and latrine buildings," and not use or enter buildings used by white personnel. Each of the one hundred and one Negro officers refused to sign and obey the order. On 13 April 1945 the 101 officers were ordered arrested by Colonel Selway, and transferred from Freeman Field, Indiana to Godman Field, Kentucky under military guard and kept under arrest at Godman Field.

Harry S. Truman became the President of United States 12 April 1945. Shortly thereafter he isued two executive orders, one setting up new machinery to halt discrimination in federal employment, the other dealing with the armed services. President Truman felt and expressed that he wanted orders regarding racial discrimination "with teeth in them and no loop holes." He further stated: "It is essential that there be maintained in the armed services of the United States the highest standards of democracy, with equality treatment and opportunity for all those who serve in our

Country's defense." Executive Order 9980 was issued to deal with civilians in federal employment and industries with federal contracts. Executive Order 9981 dealt with the military ". . . It is hereby declared to be the policy of the President that there shall be equality of treatment and opportunity for all persons in the armed services without regard to race, color, religion or national origin. . . ."

The record of the Tuskegee Airmen is documented and officially recorded as outstanding in the history of the United States archives. The brilliant records of the fighter pilots and the supporting ground crews of the 99th Pursuit Squadron and the 332nd in combat in North Africa, Sicily, and Italy was so distinguished and outstanding that the formation of other groups, i.e., 477th which was composed of bomber pilots, navigators, gunners, bombardiers, and ground crews followed. These groups established added records for American Military history in aviation that are second to none. During all escort missions in the 15th Air Force under the comand of Major General Nathan F. Twining they never lost a plane.

President Harry S. Truman awarded to the Tuskegee Airmen the Presidential Unit Citation for the unsurpassed record of destroying eighty-two enemy aircraft in one day.

THE NATIONAL AIRMEN'S ASSOCIATION
CERTIFICATE OF INCORPORATION

STATE OF ILLINOIS, COOK COUNTY

To EDWARD J. HUGHES, Secretary of State:

We, the undersigned, Cornelius R. Coffey, Dale L. White, Harold Hurd, Willa B. Brown, Marie St. Clair, Charles Johnson, Chauncey E. Spencer, Grover C. Nash, Edward H. Johnson, Janet Waterford, George Williams, and Enoc P. Waters, Jr., citizens of the United States, propose to form a corporation under an Act of the General Assembly of the State of Illinois, entitled, "An Act concerning Corporations," approved April 18, 1872, and all Acts amendatory therof; and for the purpose of such organization we hereby state as follows, to-wit:

1. The name of such corporation is THE NATIONAL AIRMEN'S ASSOCIATION OF AMERICA.

2. The object for which it is formed is . . . . to further stimulate interest in aviation, and to bring about a better understanding in the entire field of aeronautics.

3. The mangement of the aforesaid association shall be vested in a board of aviation Directors.

4. The following persons are hereby selected as the Directors to control and manage said corporation for the first year of its corporate existence, viz.:

Cornelius R. Coffey, Harlem Airport, Oak Lawn, Ill.
Dale L. White, 4358 Michigan Ave., Chicago, Ill.
Harold Hurd, 6109 Calumet Ave., Chicago, Ill.
Willa B. Brown, 5440 Indiana Ave., Chicago, Ill.
Marie St. Clair, 1102 W. 61st St., Chicago, Ill.
Charles Johnson, 1048 W. Van Buren, Chicago, Ill.

Chauncey E. Spencer, 5724 Indiana Ave., Chic., Ill.
Grover C. Nash, 6119½ Calumet Ave., Chicago, Ill.
Edward H. Johnson, 4906 Vincennes, Chicago, Ill.
Janet Waterford, 5859 Calumet Ave., Chicago, Ill.
George Williams, 5615 Prairie Ave., Chicago, Ill.
Enoc P. Waters, Jr., 3435 Indiana Ave., Chicago, Ill.

5. The location is in the city of Chicago in the county of Cook in the State of Illinois, and the post office is at No. 3435 Indiana Avenue Street in the said City of Chicago.

16th August 1939
Signed:

Cornelius R. Coffey	Chauncey E. Spencer
Dale L. White	Grover C. Nash
Harold Hurd	Edward H. Johnson
Willa B. Brown	Janet Waterford
Marie St. Clair	George Williams
Charles Johnson	Enoc P. Waters, Jr.

INFORMATIONAL SOURCES

United States Congressional Record-Seventy-Sixth Congress.

The *Chicago Defender News,* Chicago, Illinois.

The *Pittsburgh Courier* archives—Union University, Richmond, Virginia.

Enoch P. Waters, Jr., Washington, D.C.

United States Air Force, Washington, D.C., Records, Sect. of War & U.S. Air Corps.

Special Studies—*U.S. Army in World War II, The Employment Of Negro Troops,* by Ulysses Lee, Office of the Chief of Military History, United States Army.

Time Magazine—September 25, 1939.

Secretary of State's Office, State of Illinois Re: Non-Profit Cooperation Charter.

The University of Michigan, *The Chauncey Spencer Papers,* Bentley Historical Library, University of Michigan Library, Ann Arbor, Michigan.